HUMA RISING

MY JOURNEY FROM BANKRUPTCY TO BILLIONAIRE
BACK TO ASPIRING UPSTART IN THE CANNABIS INDUSTRY

P. Vincent Mehdizadeh

ISBN: 0692625305
ISBN 13: 9780692625309

Preamble

FROM THE BEGINNING of civilization, people the world over have sought natural remedies for what ailed them. Unlike its more potent and potentially dangerous cousins, cannabis has long been hailed for its therapeutic benefits—even as naysayers have attempted to outlaw and legislate it. Truly, cannabis has always had a unique place in history.

Chinese emperors are said to have used cannabis for its healing properties as far back as 2700 BC. Between 1213 and 200 BC, cannabis began to make its way into medical preparations in Egypt, India, Ancient Greece, and the Middle East. And for most herbalists practicing during the Middle Ages, hemp was a staple.

Then, thanks to the arrival of settlers, cannabis made its way to North America. It was rumored to grow alongside the tomatoes and turnips in the gardens of some of the earliest US presidents. At the end of the 1700s, Napoleon's forces reportedly transported cannabis from Egypt to France, and forty years later in the United Kingdom, cannabis extracts were secretly administered to the ailing queen. During the same time frame in the West, hemp found its way into mainstream medicine. And, by the turn of the twentieth century, cannabis was considered one of the more important medicines in India.

Thanks to their anesthetic properties, opiates began to be perceived as the new miracle drugs, welcomed by doctors and surgeons alike. By the 1870s and throughout the rest of the nineteenth century, cocaine, opiates, and other drugs were routinely used in medical preparations—despite an increase in addiction to them. Meanwhile, the cannabis plant had enjoyed an honorable reputation as a potent medicinal herb, and its therapeutic value was already well established in nineteenth-century medical literature. Pharmaceutical companies like Bristol-Myers Squibb sold it in remedies to treat a variety of ailments.

Then, on June 30, 1906, President Roosevelt signed the Wiley Act (the Pure Food and Drug Act) into law, creating the Food and Drug Administration (FDA). The FDA had the power to regulate food and drugs, and the administration's regulations caused a decline in addiction.

The twentieth century brought landmark legislation related to cannabis and hemp: the Harrison Narcotics Tax Act of 1914 prohibited the dispensation and distribution of narcotic drugs and was viewed as the model for future drug-regulation legislation. Between 1915 and 1927, ten US states passed cannabis-prohibition laws. Meanwhile, the Narcotic Drugs Import and Export Act of 1922 prohibited the import and use of opium and other narcotics except for medical purposes.

In February of 1925, cannabis resin (hashish) was included on the list of narcotics covered by the International Opium Convention sponsored by the League of Nations. Three years later, the United Kingdom followed suit, adding the drug to its list of prohibited drugs in its Dangerous Drugs Act of 1928.

By the 1930s, the hemp plant's scientific name, cannabis, was joined by a more pejorative name: marijuana. American pharmaceutical companies began responding to an increased demand for hemp-based drugs. In 1936, as schoolchildren everywhere had to watch the film *Reefer Madness*, a warning against the inevitable road to addiction that follows cannabis experimentation, the Federal Bureau of Narcotics urged federal oversight of cannabis use. In October of 1937, at the same time that the American Medical Association supported research into medical cannabis, Congress enacted the Marihuana [*sic*] Tax Act, leading to a decline in cannabis prescriptions.

That same month, Samuel R. Caldwell, an unemployed laborer from Denver, Colorado, was arrested in a raid of the Lexington Hotel, giving him the dubious distinction of being the first cannabis seller ever arrested (and the first arrest under the new federal drug law). Fined $1,000 and sentenced to four years of hard labor, he was released in 1940 and died the following summer at the age of sixty-one.

In 1978, thirty-seven years after the death of Samuel R. Caldwell and half a world away, I was born in Iran. This was during the Iranian Revolution in which Islamic fundamentalists rejected Western culture and a new regime was born. But my family would not be in its home country to face the turmoil. When I was only two years old, we emigrated to the United States.

Decades later, I would grow up and invent technology aimed at changing the way the cannabis sector ran its businesses. I founded Medbox—a company that pushed the conversation about cannabis, an amazing wonder plant, into the mainstream public's psyche. I used the media as the catalyst to spark widespread financial-industry acceptance and public change in the way the legal-cannabis industry was viewed. But before becoming wildly successful, wealthy, and prominent, I would be derided, maligned, tracked, charged with crimes I didn't commit, and left bankrupt.

Yet, proving that the American dream is alive and well, I ultimately prevailed. I overcame my obstacles and stand as living proof that we "make our own luck" and that the universe takes care of givers, not takers. But, as you will read, my story is far from over, and my true destiny has yet to be written. I titled an earlier version of this book *Self-Made: How I Became a Billionaire in the Cannabis Industry without Selling a Gram.* Considering that my stint in the elite class of about 1,600 billionaires worldwide was short-lived and because of the turmoil I currently face (which you will soon read about), titling the book *Huma Rising* seemed more apropos.

The *huma* is a legendary phoenix-like bird within Persian mythology, consuming itself in fire every few hundred years, only to rise anew from the ashes. The creature is often referred to as a bird of paradise. It is considered compassionate. It is also called a bird of fortune, since its shadow (or touch) is said to be auspicious—if it falls on a person's head or shoulder, it bestows or foretells kingship. Accordingly, the feathers decorating the turbans of ancient kings were said to be huma-bird plumage.

Thank you for purchasing my book.
All sales proceeds shall be equally distributed to the following charities: Operation Smile, St. Jude Children's Research Hospital, the ASPCA, and the Sierra Club Foundation.

CHAPTER 1

The Life Experiences That Mold Us

Purpose dictates the difference between depression and joy.

NOT ONLY HAD I just lost my mother to suicide, but the rest of my life was unraveling at the same time. As I sat at the funeral home, I was thinking, *I am in the middle of an IRS audit...my house is in foreclosure proceedings...the main source of income I've depended on for years to support myself and my parents is coming to a grinding halt...I have a criminal record...and my mother just killed herself.* On that overcast afternoon in February of 2008, in Westwood, California, the very clear thought then came to me: *I need to find a way to make my life work!*

For the rest of my life, I will associate Valentine's Day with my mother's death, since she died on that day in 2008. About four months prior, I had become very worried about her. More than ever before, she had been exhibiting signs of depression and the desire to hurt herself—and possibly even my father, who had divorced her ten years earlier. She made outlandish comments to my siblings and me about a murder-suicide fantasy in which she ended her and my father's lives and that it be a big, public spectacle. It's hard to take people seriously when they make statements like that, and it's especially difficult when it's family. My mother had been very hurt by my father's treatment of her, and some part of her wanted to punish him. She eventually took matters into her own hands and relieved herself of the pain she was feeling. Unfortunately, she robbed her children of their mother in the process.

My parents had divorced around 1997, when I was in my late teens. My mother took it very hard and understandably so. She had expected to live out the rest of her years with my father. But she wasn't always the easiest person to be around. She was very critical of him and could be very demanding. I think my father had his hands full with her. Now, he speaks of their marriage like this: "I was having a very tough time with her, and I just stayed with her because of you kids."

While I understand my father's perspective, in my opinion, the mother of a man's children should be revered and never discarded. At the very least, if a divorce is unavoidable, I think it's a man's responsibility to ensure that the ex-wife lives as well as she did when they were married. It sends a clear message to the children of the marriage that no matter what, respect is never lost between family members. Some things need to be sacred. But unfortunately, the animosity got the best of them, and after the divorce, my dad responded callously toward my mother and with a self-centered approach that was impossible for me to ignore.

My mother became very resentful and scornful toward my father, and she never really found her place after that. The Persian culture is very family oriented. You stick it out, no matter what; that's the Persian way. Without her family intact, my mother faced inner turmoil and boundless depression. We attempted to get her introduced to other eligible men, but it was difficult for her to move on…she lost her purpose.

ↄɒ

Before moving our family to the United States, my father was part of the royal cabinet of the Shah of Iran, working as undersecretary of agriculture. He had come to the States temporarily to receive a Western education at North Carolina State University, from undergraduate through doctoral degrees, before returning to Iran.

Sadly, I don't know firsthand what my home country was like, but I've heard that it was scenic and absolutely beautiful. Of course, my parents remembered all the good things about it. But there was also all the unrest that had caused the revolution. My parents held the view that the revolution had been initiated by a manipulative figure named Khomeini. He promised the people an enlightened way of living and financial security in return for rejecting Western culture and embracing a more religious and Islamic approach to life. But after the revolution was successful in overthrowing the Shah, Khomeini failed to deliver.

Iran was quickly becoming Westernized, and the entire social scene was changing and becoming more liberal. It even had fast-food restaurants. The religious fundamentalists thought that Iran being in any way similar to the United States was heretical. But my parents had always been fans of western culture, and that's what led them to move the family away—and to the States, no less.

When the revolution took place, the head of the revolutionaries put out a kill order for anyone affiliated with the former regime. As a member of the royal cabinet, my father was included. So he put my mother on a flight to London, along with my sister, brother, and me. It would have been too dangerous for him to join us on the flight. Along with others in a similar predicament, my father found a way to escape.

Meanwhile, my uncle posed as my father long enough to allow him safe passage, for which he paid with imprisonment. He remained silent about the ruse during his incarceration, but just as they were about to execute him, he finally spoke up: "You have the wrong man! I'm actually his brother..." When the revolutionaries heard this and verified my uncle's true identity, they let him go free.

It wasn't until two months after we landed in London that my father was finally able to join us. He had had to make sure the coast was clear. My father was one of the lucky ones. Several of his colleagues from the royal cabinet were captured and killed.

We lived in London for two years before emigrating to California. I was a two months old when we left Iran; my brother was ten, and my sister was fourteen. My sister and brother had it harder than I did. They were in their formative years, and it was traumatizing for them to move from one country to another and leave behind everything they knew.

When we came to the United States, my father had nothing, but thanks to a good understanding of the western business world, he was able to build a life and provide for his family by selling insurance. After holding such a prestigious and formidable position as he had in the government of Iran, my father wanted a steady, secure income. While he worked, my mother looked after the house.

My parents seemed to acclimate to Western living very easily. My father is a chameleon, and so was my mother. I, too, have learned to adapt to any situation. Everyone has chameleon-like abilities, but circumstances dictate who discovers that side of themselves. If you're never taken outside your comfort zone, you never discover your hidden ability to adapt to your surroundings, be dynamic, or do extraordinary things.

My father is a highly educated man, but he also has a tendency to take financial risks in business to hit that proverbial "home run." In the insurance field for over twenty years, he became a prominent salesman. Concurrently, he started many other businesses and other ventures that he hoped would provide more for our family, but it didn't quite work out that way. His other endeavors actually dragged us down at times.

When my father worked for the Shah of Iran, we had lived like royalty, and he seemed always to be trying to reclaim that kind of grandeur. To some extent, that's cultural—Persians in general are very status oriented. I remember when I was a child, my father came home with a *used* Rolls-Royce. The car must only have been worth sixty or seventy grand, but my father trotted it around town as a status symbol. When I asked him back then what the point was in having such a flashy car, he told me it was "good for business."

At an early age, I could see that my father enjoyed the finer things in life, and I admired that trait in him as well as his work ethic. As an adult, I see it through a different lens; now it feels like he was overreaching, trying to keep up appearances. This cultivated in me a skewed perception of money that I had to change over time so that I wouldn't find myself overreaching. In my twenties—before I learned how to properly value money—I spent most of what I made and put less into savings. That was one of the hurdles of being raised in a status-oriented family like mine. I struggled with this much of my adult life, feeling that I finally conquered that problem in my early thirties, to a certain degree.

Ironically, now that I'm worth millions of dollars, money no longer feels the same to me. I've realized that money is the means to an end but not the end itself. After everything I've been through, my real priority is to try to breeze through the rest of my life without any more traumatic events. Don't get me wrong—I enjoy being able to afford nice things, but I don't let my possessions define me as a person. Again, this understanding has come later in life for me, and I'm still working on it.

My father was always trying to keep up with everyone else and set himself apart. When we first came to California, we moved to Westlake Village, a family-oriented suburban town north of Los Angeles. We were living in a middle-class environment, but my family was always trying to jump to the upper class. My father had an office in Beverly Hills, which made him feel like he'd made it. Every day for eight years, he would make that long commute, which amounted to at least an hour each way.

Finally, my mother suggested to him, "Why don't we just buy a place closer to your office?" So, during my grade-school years, we lived in a Beverly Hills condo that my parents bought. As a kid, when you hear people talking about Beverly Hills, you envision the lavish lifestyles of the "rich and famous." But our condo was south of Wilshire Boulevard and not in the opulent section of town. All I knew then was that we lived in a nice house. I had no idea we weren't rich. The truth was we were trying to keep up with the Joneses and climb social classes.

I'm not critical of my parents for aspiring to the upper class. Persian culture is classist; it's all about what you have and what you can bring to the table. That value system was ingrained in me from an early age. Having left Iran when I was just a baby, I became westernized, and to some extent, I gravitated away from a classist perspective. But there's no question that I've always wanted to have nice cars and live in a nice house. As far as I was concerned, that's how things were *supposed* to be.

Having that mind-set ingrained in you when you're young can really affect you later on in life. When I have a family, I won't give my wife and kids a false sense of their social status. Having said that, though, I understand that I might not be as wealthy as I am today had everything not worked out exactly as it did—even my mother's death, although I would trade it all to have her back.

I had to teach myself not to see the world through a classist lens. Funnily enough, I learned a lot of my life lessons from TV sitcoms. I watched a lot of them when I was growing up, and at the end of every show, there was always a life lesson. In many ways, television raised me. My parents were there, and they provided for me and gave me nurturing and support. But I owe some of whom I've become to those lessons I learned from TV, as strange as it sounds.

Speaking of TV shows, I attended Beverly Hills High School at the height of the whole *Beverly Hills, 90210* craze. Other than some common themes like drug use, the TV school and the actual high school didn't seem to resemble each other that much. My school was just a regular high school, but because it was in a more affluent area, students had more access to money to buy "bud," as we called it—another name for cannabis.

From the time I was in grade school, I believed in nurturing the brain one was born with and refraining from doing anything that might lessen its impact on one's life. When I saw all the kids around me drinking and smoking bud, my opinion that you shouldn't damage or interfere with what you were born with faded somewhat. It wasn't so much peer pressure that led me to try bud—it was more a sense of, *Maybe this is just a social thing.*

I first tried bud in my sophomore year of high school and smoked it maybe a total of twenty to thirty times throughout all my high-school years—and I probably drank no more than once a month throughout all of high school. To put this level of frequency in perspective, you have to realize that I was surrounded by pot and alcohol almost every single weekend.

The cool kids at Beverly Hills High had parents that weren't around as often, so their homes were available for parties. I wasn't in that category of latchkey kids and didn't have an empty house to offer, but I still found ways to be accepted. Sometimes I would partake, and sometimes I wouldn't. When I did, it was always to be social and avoid being seen as an outcast. I enjoyed the effects of alcohol and bud, but I've never had an addictive personality. Whatever that genetic characteristic may be, I was not afflicted with it. I'm extremely grateful I've never had the predilection.

It was an interesting time for me because, during the latter part of my high-school experience, my parents began the divorce process. The end of their marriage was precipitated by an affair. My father had been caught being unfaithful, and things got pretty nasty between my parents. My mother was understandably hurt and outraged and never forgave my father. He escalated the situation by inviting the other woman into our lives and eventually, years later, he married her.

Before my father got caught cheating, we were a close family. "I love you" wasn't thrown around every two minutes, but I did feel loved. My father was a stern man who didn't tolerate any disrespect, but he was a good father, and we never wanted for anything. Despite my parents' arguments, I had a good childhood. The way it played out—moving from suburban Westlake Village into Beverly Hills—shaped who I am today. I have been through a lot in life, but I have never lost my upbringing and the values that went with it.

The divorce took a few long, drawn-out years during which things turned really nasty. As I said, my father married the woman with whom he'd been unfaithful, and the disrespect he had showed my mother toward the end of their marriage had a huge emotional impact upon our family. My father's affair was also a major life lesson for me and taught me what not to do when I eventually started a family of my own.

My father now expected us to accept this woman into the family, but I never truly did—especially after my mother's death. I had no connection to her at all and didn't want to accept her, since it felt to me like a betrayal of my mother. Even though I continue to support my father to the tune of thousands of dollars per month, I have taken steps to make sure that, when he's gone, this woman—now his wife—receives none of the wealth I've built. I did this out of respect to my mother, not to be vindictive.

As high-school graduation approached, there was a big crash in the real-estate market, and an investment my parents had made went sideways. By the time I began getting acceptance letters from universities, all the wealth they had built was gone. So I wasn't going to be able to accept any school invitations. I had applied to two colleges, and both had accepted me: Santa Barbara State University and Chapman University in Orange County, California. I liked both campuses and everything they brought to the table, and I liked the idea of being local to Southern California. Santa Barbara State was my first choice. But I couldn't attend either. I had to go to community college in Los Angeles instead, helping to operate a failing family side business—a lawyer-referral service that was almost a hobby for my father—while he maintained the insurance practice that paid the family's bills.

My brother and sister, being ten and fifteen years older than I was, had benefited from my parents still having money during their college years. Peyman (pronounced "pay-man") went to University of Southern California, where he got his degree in business and then earned a law degree. Sheida (pronounced "shay-duh") went to California State University, Northridge, and then to University of California, Los Angeles, for her master's in psychology. Both worked hard and earned everything they ended up with, so I'm certainly not taking anything away from them and their struggles to achieve their accomplishments. However, when it came time for me to pursue undergraduate studies, my options were severely limited due to circumstances beyond my control. That was my reality, and it was very sobering.

I was months away from graduating high school and about to start working days at the lawyer-referral office part time while attending community college a few nights per week. I had already been working two other part-time jobs during my senior year and would continue so I could help the family and pay my own bills as well. My senior-year nights were spent making smoothies at Jamba Juice and weekends at the Robinsons-May women's shoe department. It was ironic, since my parents had contributed $7,500 toward the used Porsche I bought when I was a junior; it went with the $2,500 I had saved up over the years. My brother had found the car for me. Although a 944 was considered a "poor man's Porsche" by many enthusiasts, the car was in great condition, and I was happy with it. The irony was that my junior year had started with so much promise—the purchase of my first car—but by senior year, I felt silly driving that car after my family's financial collapse.

Timing can sometimes be an important aspect of finding both success and happiness in life. Had I received the same opportunities as my siblings, I'd undoubtedly be living an entirely different life. I might have avoided some costly mistakes that would plague me in early adulthood. On the flip side of that, I doubt that I'd be as successful as I am now or living a life filled with such stimulating challenges. I'd probably be living an above-average life, content to pull in six figures a year at a corporate job somewhere, working nine-to-five and having the fruits of my labor benefit my employer. While that is a respectable approach to life, it wasn't one that I ever had a choice to pursue. At the time, I felt stuck in a version of a life that my parents had created for me as a product of their financial issues and divorce instead of the life I had otherwise been meant to have.

As senior year ended, I noticed that my friends were getting excited about their college plans. I was genuinely excited for them too and never let on that anything was problematic on my end. Every time someone asked about my situation, I simply said that I had acceptance letters for a couple of schools and was weighing my options. While I didn't like misleading my friends that I was "still deciding," the thought of divulging my family's issues to them was a nonstarter for me. Many of my friends had come from wealthy families, and it would have ruined our relationship dynamic had they realized my family was no longer doing well financially.

I might have underestimated my friends at the time, but I wasn't willing to ostracize myself unnecessarily.

About two months before graduation, I was greeted with a foreclosure notice posted on the door to the family condo. It was all too much to stomach for me at eighteen years old. The family home was in trouble. If all this weren't bad enough, I had the added burden of being asked to help make a failing family business profitable immediately without the benefit of any business experience. I realized then, at eighteen, that my life was forever changed. It was never going to be what it had been again. I had to plan for my parents' future, since my brother and sister were not in a position to help financially. I also had to figure out where I was going to live, since the bank would own the family home within months. I was breaking down mentally but didn't have enough perspective to realize it at the time.

My world was crashing down around me, and I was traumatized. But I experienced it from a distance, as if in a trance. My brother, sister, and mother would routinely ask, "You must be going through a lot!" and I'd reply, "No—I don't care. I'm tough, and I'll be OK." But internally, I was in a state of shock and denial. That's when I took a step that in retrospect I see as a major cry for help, but at the time, I was oblivious. I just wanted to change my reality in some way.

A few days later, I broke into a neighbor's condo in our complex while they weren't home. Obviously, if I'd wanted to do something illegal and get away with it, I wouldn't have chosen the condo upstairs from ours. But it was the easiest way I could find to bring attention to myself. While I couldn't have articulated it at the time, much less analyze what was behind it, I no longer wanted to deal with what was happening around me in my life. I was trying to escape it any way I could.

CHAPTER 2

— ❧ —

The Beginnings of an Aspiring Entrepreneur

<u>Have faith in doing the right thing and
operate with no fear.</u>

As I GRADUATED, the bank foreclosed upon the family house, and I was given one week to move out. My father and I stayed with my brother in his apartment, and my mother stayed with a close friend of hers. Somewhere in this same time frame, my break-in was discovered. I had done it while I was still a minor, but since I was turning eighteen when it came to light, my conviction for breaking and entering and burglary went on to my adult record.

I didn't go to jail, but I was put on probation. I was also forced to attend a six-month work-furlough program. I would go to work in the morning and early evening and then sleep nights at a private halfway house in central Los Angeles. This was a major wake-up call to both my family and me. While it's hard to pinpoint my exact mind-set at the time, in retrospect, it seems I achieved my purpose in acting out. My situation ended up galvanizing the family and forced my parents to work together to keep me from drowning. While that didn't fix their failed relationship, it redirected everyone's attention away from the larger issues, a much-needed distraction for the family at that point.

At last, the six months came to an end. Already having a felony on my record at such a young age, I felt like I was on my own in deep water without any sort of flotation device. I was either going to sink or swim. Fortunately, I swam. I didn't let having a criminal record affect me. I knew in my heart I wasn't a criminal—I was just a victim of circumstances. My life had led me to make a bad choice as a means of alerting my parents to the fact that I was drowning internally because I had been forced to endure the results of their problems. It took me years after that to piece it all together and see it with clarity.

When I was released from the work-furlough program, I needed to find an apartment. To make ends meet, I strung together a few jobs. Like a junior Al Bundy from *Married with Children*, I resumed working in the women's shoe department at Robinsons-May. Some nights and on weekends, I sold clothes at a Rodeo Drive store named Bernini. My father's lawyer-referral service work was my third job. I attended community college every Tuesday and Thursday evening. All this took up an average of seventy hours a week. I needed to feel I was making a positive financial impact on the family while driving myself forward in the process. Achieving goals was always a priority for me and gave me the initiative to plow forward under tough circumstances.

In 1990, my father had reached the point where he needed to develop other revenue streams for the family besides his insurance business. He established the referral service when he met an attorney who gave him the idea; he began with partners and then bought them out over the years. The business was certified by the State Bar of California to refer qualified attorneys to the public.

When I got on board, my father had been running the business with his receptionist, but it wasn't properly developed or marketed. It was just treading water, barely bringing in $3,000 a month—only enough to cover the rent, the bar's annual certification fees, and part of the receptionist's salary. The business was really an afterthought—it had been overlooked as my father focused on his core business.

I was only nineteen, but I made developing the business my focus. We had about sixty attorneys in various disciplines, like family, criminal, and civil law, registered with us. If the general public needed a licensed, insured, prescreened attorney, they turned to us. At my age, I found it a little overwhelming to speak to attorneys at first, but I threw myself into it and began to gain confidence. I started marketing different products to the attorneys on our roster and trying to come up with unique ways of getting them cases. In general, attorneys are a very skeptical group of people and tough to close on abstract ideas.

For the first few years, I continued to run the business the way it had been set up. As its director, my father was in the office with me, overseeing my work. Though I had to run everything by him, the business was really my baby, as he was busy with his own. It was a learning experience, trying to market our services to new attorneys and talking to existing ones about why they should renew with us for an annual $180. This was my very first introduction to the business world—my informal, "crash-course" business degree.

We had an endless array of potential clients who all needed help. But, by the third year, I started noticing that there was a certain group of people who called in for referrals but didn't receive the assistance they needed. These were lower-income families and people living on fixed incomes who were being sued for one reason or another. We referred them to one of the few attorneys that had agreed to participate in our reduced-fee panel, but the fee was often still too high for the potential client. Almost always, these clients, who couldn't afford an hourly rate or our reduced-fee panel, got turned away and sent to Legal Aid, a public legal-assistance service for indigent individuals. However, they turned out to make too much money to qualify for Legal Aid and were turned away within seconds of phoning in, at times. It's truly amazing what is considered to be over the poverty level in this country.

I knew there were plenty of people in that boat. It seemed completely unfair for these families to be facing bankruptcy because they couldn't afford to fight claims against them. And it didn't seem right to have attorneys charging $5,000 initial retainers and billing $300 per hour with no end in sight for when the case might be resolved and the bills ceased. Potential clients would say, "OK, we can put four or five thousand dollars on a credit card." But when the fee later included another $4,000 to $5,000, they couldn't come up with the money. The attorneys had no choice but to withdraw from representation, and the clients were left midway through a case without counsel. That's actually worse than never having counsel in the first place.

For example, a cable company was suing one family for having an illegal cable box. It was a ridiculous lawsuit, considering that the family claimed that a uniformed cable-company employee had come out to their house and *offered* them the box. They had no reason to suspect that it was illegal. The purported employee encouraged the family to pay for it in cash, saying that this would expedite the service. The family took this request at face value and did as he asked. Now, the family was looking at defending a costly civil suit. They had no funds to pay an attorney an initial retainer and then ongoing fees until the case was resolved, so they were contemplating bankruptcy and asked us for a referral for that.

I thought that many of these issues could be handled on a flat-fee basis, but a lot of attorneys don't like those because there's no telling how long they'll need to work a case. I've met my fair share of honest attorneys, but I've also seen firsthand that some like to fan a case's flames just to churn more billable hours. That left me frustrated. So I decided to offer flat-fee services to help resolve these kinds of cases without going over the initial retainer quotes.

In the course of doing business, I'd met a few attorneys who needed clients and were interested in working with me. I decided to approach one named Frank, who was already qualified to receive our referrals. "Frank," I said, "look, I realize you can't necessarily ensure a flat fee of four or five thousand dollars because of your billable hours in going to court, preparing filings, and things like that. But what if I worked in your office as a legal assistant? I could learn the ropes, and I'd handle all this work. We could take care of these clients who are otherwise falling through the cracks." Frank agreed, and with that, a partnership was born.

The California State Bar had certain rules governing attorney-referral services. One rule was that you couldn't be employed by both a law office and a referral service because of conflict of interest. I decided to separate myself from the referral service and work for this attorney, who was willing to give my idea a shot. Someone else was assigned to answer the phones and issue referrals to keep the service in compliance with the state-bar's standards. This arrangement continued under the supervision of my father. When callers said they preferred a flat fee, they were routed to me.

When the model started to prove successful, I quit my retail jobs and focused fully on community college and the law office, which had begun to pay tens of thousands of dollars in referrals to our service. The afterthought family business was now supporting the family under this revamped business model.

Immediately, I could see that the flat-fee model was helping people. In the illegal cable-box case, for example, our office accepted a $2,000 flat fee and resolved the issue within two months through a walk-away settlement. The family simply signed an agreement with the cable company that it would never be tricked into using an illegal cable box again. In my opinion, that was a fair resolution. The family brought us a cake at the office to celebrate. We had saved them from filing for bankruptcy! Bottom line: the office was yielding results because I had a no-nonsense approach to it all and worked with the attorney to resolve cases as quickly as possible because they were all on a flat-fee basis. It was simply a more economical approach for the law office, and the clients were elated that their matters were handled so swiftly and within their quoted amounts.

The other state-bar rule prohibited an attorney-referral service from referring more than 20 percent of cases to any one firm. The thinking was, it was better to spread the work around: all attorneys participating in the program would get referrals. There was no criminal penalty if a service violated those rules; however, if a violation was discovered, the service would be decertified. We stayed in compliance.

I continued working as Frank's office manager and legal assistant under this system for the next five years: our flat-fee office offered clients a legitimate service, we followed all the state-bar rules, and in our minds, there was no conflict. I figured that these people would not be getting helped otherwise.

From 2003 to 2006, the business thrived. We got many clients from word-of-mouth referrals, and that doesn't happen unless you offer a good service. Frank was very much involved, and I appreciated that he took a strong interest in what was going on. I learned the ins and outs of a myriad of legal facets. The tools I now have at my disposal were drawn from experience I gathered while managing law offices back in the day. Those experiences taught me how to think analytically, gave me the ability to think on my feet and problem solve, and allowed me to develop my business intuition.

CHAPTER 3

Careless Attorneys and the Aftermath

<u>The more you have, the more you have to lose.</u>

FRANK WAS A good attorney to learn from, but he had issues that led to me ending our working relationship. Along with his success and wealth came a cocaine habit, and I felt like his clients suffered as a result. He was a genuinely nice guy when he wasn't partaking in his vices. In his defense, he did warn me ahead of time about these tendencies, which at the time he had stifled; he had been sober for about a decade. So when his addiction came back and began to impact the business, I wasn't completely taken by surprise.

I realized that I needed to find a more stable attorney for the clients' benefits as well as my own. Once Frank forced himself out of the picture through his destructive behavior, I had to go scouting for someone else to run the firm. Enter "Tom," an attorney whose practice was primarily drafting wills and trusts. We had a preexisting relationship; he had been receiving referrals from our other service for years.

There were two reasons I agreed to work with Tom. For one thing, I was anxious to get the office up and running again so we could continue helping clients that needed low-cost and fixed-fee representation. I also liked the fact that he seemed willing to work within the parameters I'd already set up. Many other attorneys were opportunists. They were way too aggressive moneywise and tended to want to alter the flat-fee business model for their benefit, which contradicted the point and simply wouldn't have worked.

When I met Tom, he was a bit down on his luck and open to a steady paycheck in whatever form. He was in his midfifties, Caucasian, and distinguished-looking with gray hair. He had a pleasant demeanor and was very knowledgeable, and he took me under his wing. I very much appreciated his guidance.

In early 2006, I began working for Tom's office as a legal assistant and director of client relations. I attended meetings with clients who came to us through the referral service, and clients were signing retainers regularly. Everything was done with Tom's complete involvement. But he was taking a very lazy approach to our business, only coming into the office three times a week to look over the files. I felt the clients weren't being adequately looked after. So I took the initiative to arrange paralegal and attorney hiring meetings and urged Tom to pull the trigger on hiring more staff. By 2007, the office had hired full-time paralegals and two full-time attorneys to manage cases. I felt comfortable that I was fulfilling my promise to the clients of competent legal representation. Tom was happy about it too, but it generally seemed like an afterthought for him.

I had no way of knowing the real reason that Tom was taking such a lax approach with our office. Then, through a fluke, I came to find out why. He had two other offices, just like ours, set up in other parts of the city! This fact came to light entirely by accident in late 2007. One day, Tom inadvertently brought to my attention an issue related to a client with whom I was unfamiliar—one who hadn't originated from our Beverly Hills office. Tom wasn't paying attention and thought the client was one of ours. When I pressed the point, he admitted to having other offices.

I considered this a betrayal. Tom was putting our office at risk by spreading himself too thin. There was also the potential that his business practices at the other firms could have a spillback effect on our Beverly Hills office. He was not using the flat-fee model in those other offices—he was running different services, and I wasn't privy to the details. Had I known of Tom's other offices, I wouldn't have worked with him to the degree I had.

I'd begun working with Tom in early 2006, and by the end of 2006, he had a tax lien on his other business accounts that made its way into our Beverly Hills office's business account. I walked into the office one day and discovered that the Internal Revenue Service (IRS) had debited about $60,000 from it. I confronted Tom immediately. "The firm has absolutely nothing in its operating account!"

His response was, "Oh, I'm sorry—this looks like a tax levy. I thought my tax attorney took care of this."

I said, "Well, apparently, he didn't. Get this resolved right away!"

He didn't make any offer of getting the money back. "Once the IRS zaps the money, it's gone, and there's no way of recovering it," he sheepishly stated. I felt bad for Tom, who came across as a likeable guy down on his luck. I was still very naive.

Either we were going to have to close our doors, or I was going to have to loan the company money. I was working seventy hours a week, and I had a modest nest egg—$100,000 in personal savings. I took half the money and loaned it to the company. This was a big financial hit for me—totally unexpected.

I told Tom, "This can't ever happen again!" Then I set up a management corporation to pay all the company expenses—a move that could have protected us from the tax lien had it already been in place. I would never recoup the $60,000 we lost, but the management company ensured that this problem never arose again.

From then on, all client funds were received into the management account, and Tom's firm contracted with my management company. Tom's fee was paid from that management account, as was his staff, the rent, and other office expenses. I was now fully invested into the firm and took over more control of the finances—out of necessity, not desire.

The management relationship under which the firm was now operating was not common but also not illegal. Some attorneys are not great at managing finances, and as a result, they hire management companies to handle the day-to-day financial operations of their firms.

As if matters had not been bad enough, by late 2007 I also found out that Tom was on probation with the state bar. A potential client came into the office and said to me, "The supervising attorney in this office has a disciplinary record!" I was floored. Imagine trying to manage existing clients and attract new ones, but you can't because clients become aware of a problem like this. It made our office look less than credible and put me in an untenable position. On one hand, I was the one carrying all this responsibility, but on the other, I was only the office manager. I could not take the onus on myself and facilitate a change, since it was Tom's firm. He was the attorney.

I again confronted him. "I'm still licensed to practice law," he answered. "So this is not a concern at all. This is an issue from the past that has nothing to do with this office." Since our staff attorneys had no disciplinary issues with the bar, I rationalized that things were going to be OK. For the sake of the existing clients and the staff, we kept the office running with Tom's assistance. Given the circumstances, we began slowing our intake of new clients to prioritize existing clients and case completion.

The situation didn't become truly problematic until early 2008. That's when Tom walked into the office one day and said he was no longer able to meet the terms of his state-bar probation. In lieu of being disbarred, he had decided to voluntarily retire from the practice of law. While the issues had arisen over dealings that *predated* my business relationship with Tom, his retirement would impact my life to an extent I couldn't have begun to imagine at the time.

Tom asked the office staff to notify all our clients that he was retiring. He had put us in a difficult situation and had also violated his responsibility to the clients. They had trusted us to handle their cases until completion, but now, some would be left unfinished. Tom didn't seem to care. And since he had been the attorney of record, our other attorneys didn't want to step in and take over his cases. He was the one with direct responsibility to the clients—not me, the paralegals, or the other attorneys. His signature was on all the client retainers.

Since we had already toned down the business and accepted fewer new clients, by Tom's retirement, the business was barely earning enough to pay the salaries of our legal staff. We could not refund the clients who were left with unfinished cases.

Tom's response to the disaster he had created was, "Let them complain to the state bar. It will reimburse them." I didn't feel comfortable with that so-called solution, but my hands were tied since he was the attorney of record on all the cases. He wanted to close the doors of his office, and there was nothing more I could say or do about it. I had no choice.

Per Tom's instructions, two of the firm's paralegals and I sent out the retirement announcements to our clients, along with the files for those whose cases were unfinished so they could hire other counsel. I sent out so much certified mail that the post-office charges came to about $700.

I knew perfectly well that if clients with unfinished cases felt aggrieved, they might file complaints with the state bar, which has a fund for returning money in such instances. I also knew that they could potentially file civil suits against Tom himself as well as against his law office. There was nothing I could do about that. It was out of my hands. Now that Tom's office was closed, I no longer had any money coming in, and I was under a lot of pressure to earn a steady income.

In addition to my own monthly expenses, I was giving financial assistance to my parents. I'd been doing that since the divorce with all three of my jobs, paying my father's mortgage and supplementing my mother's alimony—which just wasn't paying her bills. The award had been only about $1,300 per month. My father said he couldn't afford to give her anything extra. I wished the court had awarded her more or my father had given more voluntarily, but the amount had been set, and I didn't really question it.

I felt I had no choice but to supplement my mother's alimony. She deserved to live comfortably, and what she was getting just wasn't cutting it, even with her monthly $500 assistance from Social Security. I came in with another $1,000 (which I later raised to $2,000). I didn't mind. Even though it was tough for me because I wasn't earning that much either, I felt she needed it.

In January of 2008, I started helping my father, who was over his head on the house he'd purchased. His insurance business was not paying as much as it once had, and with the slowing of referrals to Tom's office down to almost nothing, the referral-service revenue I had structured for my father to collect was drying up. Every case that Tom's office had signed up came from our service, up to the state bar's allowed 20 percent of the Service's referrals. This relationship had helped my father to pay his bills, including my mother's alimony, for years after our family's financial collapse. I started giving him $6,000 each month toward his mortgage and my mother's alimony.

My father responded to my financial assistance very differently than my mother did. My mother felt like she was a burden, and I had to insist that she accept my support. My father would never feel that way. He is a very proud man, but he's oblivious to a certain degree. His attitude was more grandiose: "Of course you'd take care of me! I'm your father." He would always say it with an innocent smile on his face, and I couldn't help but chuckle. Part of navigating the world around you is always under-standing the people you interact with and not being surprised when they act the way they act. People are who they are, and being upset about things you can't control is a waste of time and energy. I know that if my fa-ther had the money, he would never accept money from me. But without money yet still being proud, it's easier for him to accept help from me if he deflects attention away from the fact that he needs it.

After the closure of Tom's office in 2008, there was about a four-month stretch where I struggled and couldn't give my father his $6,000 a month. I felt horrible about not being able to come through. He didn't put any extra pressure on me, though, and I got back on track with the payments as soon as I could.

Obviously, with all the help I've given my father over the years, he's in a better place in his life. I'm glad he can live out his twilight years in peace instead of always struggling financially, and I don't mind helping him. I never forget where he came from and what he had to do to create a life for his family here. He came to the United States as someone who had enjoyed a high social status in Iran and then had to rebuild himself from scratch and find a way to support his family. That couldn't have been easy.

On the other hand, at the time, I felt like some really big problems had converged at once. For seven years, I had successfully found a way to guide my parents and me through financial hardship and actually live a very comfortable life against all odds. Now, I was once again faced with carrying the weight of my parents' financial needs and finding a new revenue stream to support us. It's not surprising that I found myself with an enormous debt to the IRS. It was a function of earning money at a young age and not having proper support from a certified public accountant (CPA). The accountants I was working with at the time weren't as meticulous as I needed them to be, and they hadn't documented my business deductions correctly. This error on their part, and mine in not realizing it, resulted in tax audits from 2003 through 2007. This meant I would have to review five years of financial documents and forensically account for every deduction my accountants had used when preparing my taxes.

Then there was the issue with a house I had purchased in 2006. In 2003, I'd bought a condo near Beverly Hills for about $200,000, with $150,000 being financed by a mortgage lender. I was thrilled to be able to make such a purchase at the age of twenty-three. The money had come as a result of hard work and savings for years. By 2006, the condo had accumulated a lot of value. So, I sold it at the height of the real-estate boom and moved into an apartment. I lived there for six months while I kept an eye on the real-estate market. When I saw the market maintaining, I decided to buy a beautiful four-bedroom house in Lake Hollywood—not far from Universal Studios. Once again, it felt like quite an accomplishment to be able to buy such a fantastic house at my age. I purchased at the height of the market in early 2007, before the housing bubble burst, for about $700,000.

The house was three years old, and I bought from the original owner. It passed inspection, and I didn't give it another thought. I had no idea what was happening inside the walls until 2008, when my dogs and I started to get sick. Suddenly, my usually playful pups were lethargic and subdued. And I'd lost the motivation to go to work for a few days, which was completely unlike me. I never took time off and steadily worked a sixty-hour workweek for years prior to that, so I knew something was up.

When I had the veterinarian look at the dogs, he told me they were having respiratory issues, and he mentioned there might be an issue with mold. I was experiencing lethargy and skin irritation, but I wasn't yet having respiratory symptoms. But I thought, *Well, whatever the dogs are inhaling is probably affecting me too.* So, after I got the dogs diagnosed, I saw the doctor myself, and sure enough, I received the same diagnosis: my symptoms were likely a reaction to mold.

I had a mold expert come out to the house. Since the house was still fairly new, I had figured it would be safe from such issues. Nothing could have been further from the truth. Here's what happened: the architect and contractor had failed to build the roof properly. Rain collected in puddles on it instead of channeling away, which weakened it. Eventually, water trickled into the walls and down three stories, affecting the entire structure. Pouring the last of my savings into the mold issue and the closure of Tom's office left me unable to afford my mortgage payment. By the end of 2008, I found myself living in a hotel and driving a rental car while trying to figure out my next move in business so I could continue to survive and support my parents.

CHAPTER 4

—— ✥ ——

The Family Ties That Bind Us Can Also Break Us

Stay positive, maintain focus, and reject negativity in all its many forms.

IT WAS MID-February of 2008, and I hadn't heard from my mother in days. I'd left several messages on her voicemail and soon got a recording saying it was full. She hadn't mentioned that she was planning to travel. I had a sneaking suspicion that something was not right.

My mother and I had a standing date every Wednesday evening after I got off work. I'd pick up a light dinner for her at a local eatery and take it to her apartment—a place I'd found for her within three blocks of my office. We'd sit down together and have a conversation over dinner.

My mother was known in the Persian community in Los Angeles as a strikingly beautiful and charming woman. Back in the day, she had been considered model pretty, with her blondish hair and green eyes. She loved the bright, floral colors popular in Persian culture, and I used to joke that she dressed like a beach ball. That was my mother—she loved being the center of attention.

From time to time, her depressive side would rear its head. When her own father died, for example, she took it very hard, crying inconsolably for weeks. Her mercurial moods made interactions with her unpleasant at times, and my brother and sister would go through stages where they didn't really want to deal with her. While I couldn't blame them because of her verbally abusive tendencies, I felt, as the youngest son, I needed to stay close to her. And, for the most part, I did. I realized early on that my mother was a product of her environment and that the things she said were not her true feelings but her resentment and anger toward my father manifested outwardly at others around her. She couldn't yell at my father, so she yelled at us. That was her reality and the reality that the ones who loved her had to endure.

When she was in a good mood, she was her usual charming, lovely self, and we'd have a great visit. Over time, our visits became alarming to me, as her side of the conversation was turning more and more morbid. On Wednesdays, I never knew whether I was going to find the charming and lovely version of my mom or the angry, bitter, resentful version of her who would say things like, "You're probably just like your dad!"

As I've noted, my mother felt like she was a burden, and she didn't want to depend on me financially anymore. Perhaps more compelling was the fact that she felt like she had nothing to live for any longer; no one needed her. She was divorced, and all three of us kids were grown. She thrived when she felt needed, and I think that's what ended up derailing her life—she lost her sense of purpose. She never really got over my dad, and being a Persian divorcee was especially hard. It's uncommon in our culture for an older woman to remarry.

I had a very bad feeling about my mother's state of mind, and I approached my family with my concerns. Since I spent the most time with my mom, I was the one to notice the signs. I picked up the phone and called both Peyman and Sheida, my siblings. Then I arranged to talk to my maternal uncle in person. I told each of them about my mother's recent mental state, and let them know I felt she was close to ending her life. I said, "Look, we have to spend more time with Mom. She's been telling me she's not feeling well, and I can tell how depressed she is. We have to do something!"

Since our mother had threatened suicide before and never followed through with it, my brother, sister, and uncle had learned to tune her out. When I talked to them, everyone reassured me, "Oh, don't worry...she'd never do such a thing…she'll be fine…she loves herself too much…she's too beautiful." They didn't take my warning seriously. Then again, they had their own lives to deal with. Situations like this are not common in most families. There is no rule that everyone knows on how to deal with a suicidal member of the family except to show her love and attention, which all of them did in their own way.

My brother, sister, and uncle rose to the occasion to a certain extent, but none of them spent enough time with my mother or made her a big enough part of their lives. I was also guilty of not doing enough. If I had it to do over again, I'd take her on trips and spend more time with her. Part of me also blamed my father for my mother's death because I felt like he hadn't been strong enough to stay with her. Another part of me understands that everyone has to live their own lives, and if they're not happy, a change might be needed to reverse that. My father doesn't get an A on the report card of life for failing to stick it out with my mother, but he doesn't get a failing grade either. He raised good kids and did his best under difficult circumstances.

That Wednesday at our usual meeting time, I rang Mom, but she didn't pick up. So I went to her apartment, which was on the ground floor, and slipped in through the kitchen window. I tiptoed from room to room, not knowing what I might find. When I walked into her bedroom, I found a bunch of stuff laid out on the bed—a note, a tape recorder and cassette, a gun case without the gun inside, and other odds and ends.

I started reading the note. "I want to thank Pej [a nickname she used for me] for keeping me alive and taking care of me…"

Mom's note went on to say she'd taken off…she didn't want to commit suicide inside the apartment…there were young mothers living there, and she didn't want to upset them…she didn't want to create a "Beverly Hills scandal" that would end up in the local news…she had decided to drive elsewhere. The note didn't say where.

Then I found a note addressed to my brother, Peyman, indicating that he should listen to the tape in the recorder. I didn't read the private note to Peyman or listen to the tape. I called Peyman, told him what was going on, and said, "You need to get over here immediately." Then I called Sheida, my uncle, and the police.

My brother arrived first and found me sitting in the living room. When he went into the bedroom, he saw everything scattered on the bed and closed the door. He privately read my mother's note to him and listened to the tape.

My brother and I have had strained relations at times, and he and my mother did, as well. She often got on his case for various things. Even though Peyman appreciated me for taking care of our mother, I know he wished he could do more for her financially. Even though my brother is older, he wasn't the one taking care of my parents financially, and at times, I felt he had mixed feelings about that and that it affected our relationship. It was a familiar subplot that we have never discussed to this day.

The night of my mother's disappearance, my family and I went through security footage at her apartment building. We discovered that she had driven off with a suitcase, so we were hoping that maybe it was a cry for help and she hadn't actually done anything to hurt herself. We started looking around, trying to find out where she'd gone. Meanwhile, the police put out an all-points bulletin on the car. About forty-eight hours later, we got a call from the police, letting us know they'd found the car. The news wasn't good. They told us, "You need to come claim the body."

So I picked up Sheida and drove about an hour north to a monastery in the Lancaster area. Peyman and my uncle met us there. My mother must have figured she'd gone far enough away from Beverly Hills that her suicide wouldn't end up broadcasted on the local evening news. In her note, she had said there was nothing left to accomplish in her life and that she had successfully raised her children. That's when I realized that she had lost her sense of purpose—a dangerous mind-set for anyone.

My mother had died of a self-inflicted gunshot wound to the head. Peyman and my uncle identified her. I chose not to see her body because I did not want that image in my mind. I wanted to remember her as she had been. We passed a very difficult night in Lancaster with the police. In the early-morning hours, we drove back to Los Angeles.

Part of me was upset with my mother for robbing us of the matriarch of the family and for robbing herself of what was going to be a happy family one day if we'd only stuck with it and persevered. It pains me because I know my mother would have loved to see the success I ultimately achieved. It would have been fantastic for her to see what I've accomplished while still in her physical form, and I believe she does see it from up above. If my mother had remained in the realm of the living, who knows if I would have been this successful and be in a position to positively impact people's lives? I firmly believe that the ones that have loved us and are no longer living are our guardian angels throughout our lives.

A week later, it was time to get up and give my speech at the funeral. Both Peyman and Sheida were adamant about me avoiding the word "suicide" in my speech. There were outsiders in attendance who were openly judgmental, and this affected my brother and sister more deeply than it did me. In Persian culture, it's all about putting on the best face possible, and they wanted to divert attention from the fact that our mother had taken her own life. I can't fault them for feeling this way. Everyone has his or her own way of dealing with trauma and tragedy. For me, suppressing the truth wasn't an option. Being honest about what had happened was part of my healing process.

People tend to think it's cowardly to commit suicide, but there's also another perspective. It takes a lot of guts and a ton of conviction to kill yourself, whether you pull the trigger of a gun or do it by other means. I obviously don't support suicide by any stretch of the imagination but realize that a person who sees no other way must be in a whole lot of pain to take his or her own life and subject loved ones to the anguish that ensues.

I got up and spoke from the heart, saying, "My mother died of a broken heart. She tried her best, but she never really got over the divorce." My father was not there to hear my words; we hadn't invited him. I continued, "And, as she said in her note, she didn't want to be a burden on me anymore. I was taking care of her financially. Now she's in a better place, and I'm in a better place because she's looking out for me, and all of us.

29

The people we've lost in our lives that have loved us are our guardian angels..."

I usually prefer to speak off the cuff, but this speech was important to me, so I'd written it down. I was recently asked to speak at Chapman University in Orange County—ironically, one of the two universities that had accepted me, but I couldn't afford to attend. One of my good friends has an in-law who is a student there, and that's how I came to be asked to speak. When I spoke at Chapman, I had nothing prepared. But there was no way I was going to wing my mother's eulogy. I gave it a great deal of advance thought and made sure I hit all the important points. "She was a beloved mother, and she loved her children..."

By the time I'd finished speaking, I felt a sense of relief. After I sat down, I again reflected on everything that had happened. Life had taken on a surreal quality. Our family matriarch had killed herself, and my siblings and I were left to pick up the pieces. My mother died at sixty-five—my smart, beautiful mother who had passed her gorgeous green eyes on to me. I could hardly believe my mother was gone, and I was only twenty-eight years old. It was hard to comprehend that someone who could be so passionate about life had committed suicide.

On top of everything else on my shoulders, I had to carry the lion's share of the financial responsibility for the funeral. I have had to accept that I am usually the one that has to step up financially in family situations. It's always been that way, and I've made peace with it. At the end of the day, I've always relished the opportunity to provide. Either I offer or it's expected of me, and it's always had a positive effect on my life. I tend to put pressure on myself to make things happen for my family and me when they need to so we can get through financial difficulties and life hurdles.

The desire to take care of my family made me a more aggressive businessman than I might otherwise have been. The tendency landed me in hot water at times. On the other hand, without my invention and the company that followed years later—Medbox—I too would have had a rougher road to success or might never have hit my stride in business.

Now that my mother was gone and her funeral was over, I was left with a pressing question: How was I to turn my life around? I started by settling my issues with the IRS for the years 2003 through 2007. This resulted in a few hundred thousand dollars in business expenses that I could not write off, plus penalties and interest that ballooned the amount I supposedly owed to $2.1 million. I didn't have a tax attorney or CPA at the time because I couldn't afford it. As tax professionals later explained to me, it was a huge mistake for me to agree to the IRS's proposed changes to my returns, but I just wanted to get the matter resolved and move on with my life.

The rest of 2008 would prove to be one of the toughest times of my life to that point. I lost my house, my cars, and my businesses. I lived in a hotel and drove a rental car for months while I regrouped. Amid all the turmoil, I never lost my focus. I was driven, and I had a sense of purpose. I was OK.

Knowing that my mother was going to be looking down on me from above for the rest of my life, I wanted to do things that she would be proud and happy to see. She used to tell me all the time, "I'm proud of you, Pej. I'm really proud of you." Of course, when she was hurt, she would make unkind comments and strike out at the ones closest to her. And when she was unbalanced and in a certain state of mind, she'd compare me to my father. But I knew those unkind words came from a hurt place, and I tried not to take it personally—easier said than done, as many children with similar stories will admit. After her death, it was easier to compartmentalize my memories of her and only remember the good.

CHAPTER 5

—— ✂ ——

Opportunities, Allegations, Redemption, and Skeletons

It doesn't matter what something is; it matters what something appears to be. Perception dominates reality most of the time...

DURING THE TIME I was managing Tom's law firm in late 2007, I needed to diversify my income. So I opened two cannabis dispensaries in Los Angeles and ran them for six months. That's when I made an interesting observation: patients seemed to derive tremendous benefits from using cannabis for medicinal purposes, but the industry itself had glaring weaknesses that could be exploited by those who didn't have the right intentions.

In my six months of interaction with various aspects of the industry, I had had experience with dispensary patients and operators, and I also understood it from the perspective of state governments, legislators, and law enforcement. In putting all the puzzle pieces together and evaluating the big picture, I noticed that critical pieces were missing.

It occurred to me that for medical cannabis to be treated fairly as a medication, a system was necessary for regulating its dispensation, much like the pharmaceutical industry had. In addition, I saw the need for safety measures to ensure that the right patient was getting the drug in the proper dosage, dosage limits weren't being breached, and physician authorization was valid and not expired. If you could put all these facets in place, then law enforcement and government officials could rest assured that no improprieties had occurred at a dispensary.

I envisioned a game-changing apparatus—for me and for the entire medical-cannabis industry. What could be better than a machine that acted as an internal auditor without stealing, taking breaks, or requiring a salary?

I didn't have an engineering background, so I did what any entrepreneur would do. I reworked an existing idea so that it met my specifications. That's always simpler than trying to reinvent the wheel. With my vision in mind, I immediately searched for companies that specialized in customized vending machines.

I filed my patent application in December of 2007 and started doing press interviews after the machine prototype was created. The idea of a machine that dispenses cannabis via fingerprint recognition had a lot of "sizzle," and it really grabbed the attention of the press. There was no question that I had a decent idea, but I also had to contend with the stigma that surrounds medical cannabis.

My initial thought process went something along these lines: I'd get these machines built, and one day, eventually, they would be mass-produced for dispensaries for a very discreet way of getting medicine to patients in an automated manner and without human interaction, if that was their choice. The dispensary would benefit because the proprietors could demonstrate that they complied with all applicable state laws and regulations in their transactions, and taxes could also be documented more efficiently. I viewed it as a win/win situation for all parties concerned.

Years later, when I actually started publicly selling the machines, my vision changed. I didn't feel that society was ready for self-service cannabis machines, even though my patent covered that type of configuration. So, I started putting the machines behind dispensary counters, accessible only by employees. We marketed the machines as safes that dispensed medicine. I also developed point-of-sale software that verified every transaction before medicine could be accessed and handed to the patient.

The system had many benefits for three main demographics: the patients' medicine was stored in a sterile, light-deprived, and temperature-controlled environment that promoted freshness; dispensary operators could monitor their inventory more effectively and also ensure that every transaction was compliant to their local/state laws; and law enforcement and state regulators would feel confident that the dispensaries had a method of operating that reduced abuse, mitigated diversion to non-medical users, and tracked taxation more effectively. I knew the product would be successful because it seemed to address most of my areas of concern in the industry.

I had no problem finding a company to create a machine that aligned with my vision and specifications. I documented everything to protect my intellectual property and went full speed ahead. A couple of months later, I got my prototype machine, and my project was born. I installed it at my Herbal Nutrition Center (HNC). I also operated a dispensary called Melrose Quality Pain Relief in Hollywood.

One day while I was working at Tom's firm, I got a call from the manager at HNC. "CBS News is here on site, and they want to do an interview about the machine! They are about to interview me."

I was very concerned and didn't want him saying the wrong thing, so I told him to hold off until I got there. I was fighting a 102-degree fever and was wearing a hoodie to keep away the chills; this was when I had the mold infestation at my house. The only reason I'd gone into work at all was to take care of a few things that couldn't wait, and without me there, the staff attorneys and paralegals had less motivation to get stuff done. I was dressed totally inappropriately for an interview, but what could I do?

There was no time to run home and switch into a suit. So I had Jeff, one of our paralegals, come with me because he was already wearing a suit. I told him, "I'm going to try to avoid the camera at all costs. So, if they need someone to speak as a representative for the dispensary, you'll have to step up."

As soon as the interview got underway, the reporter started asking questions that I needed to address, and I ended up having to hop in front of the camera. Jeff also gave his perspective by fielding some questions on camera. When the interview aired, it played well (other than that I wasn't dressed properly).

That interview led to others with more major media outlets, including CNN. In 2007, I was picked up by limousine and taken to the CNN studios on Sunset Boulevard for a live discussion on air. Interviews with Reuters and the Associated Press followed. Needless to say, in all the interviews after CBS, I appeared in a suit and tie.

The reporters conducting these interviews seemed to understand the benefits of my invention. The machine, which was still self-service at that time, offered a convenient delivery method. It sat in a room at the dispensary where preregistered users could access it during store hours with a security card and thumbprint scan. They could choose and receive their medicine in a discreet environment without waiting in line. We also offered twenty-four-hour access for some registered patients; we had a licensed security guard on site at all times to ensure their safety.

When these interviews were taking place, I was becoming very cognizant of the fact that the Bush administration was organizing raids on California dispensaries. Inevitably, they would see these interviews. As each one aired, I thought about how the Drug Enforcement Agency (DEA) was probably thinking that the machine was a bad idea because cannabis was a federally banned substance. I knew they didn't approve of the medical-cannabis industry and wouldn't understand what I was trying to do. Every time I was interviewed, the media got an opposing viewpoint from the DEA, asking them how they planned to react to this guy who seemed to be flaunting his new pot-dispensing invention. I'm sure they were irritated by this question the first time they were asked, and with each subsequent interview I did, I imagine they just became progressively more agitated.

Thinking back on the situation, even at the time, I never took a brazen or cavalier attitude about it. I fully realized that I was on a path I couldn't turn back from even if I wanted to. I also realized I was on a collision course with the DEA. Although part of me was scared, I figured that the idea behind the invention was to promote transparent operation in dispensing medical cannabis, and that if my intentions remained pure, I was part of the solution and never part of the problem; the DEA would not harm me.

With that being said, I imagine they didn't like the way my invention was being sensationalized, and quite honestly, even with the federal government's position at the time on the cannabis industry, I never had an antigovernment or counterculture sensibility. I simply felt that I was helping bring balance to an industry that needed it. My machine was providing much-needed oversight and control.

At that time, the Bush administration seemed completely intolerant of the medical-cannabis industry. They seemed to want it eradicated and considered anything related to it an abomination. I also realized there was a chance that the benefits my machine provided were of no interest to them. My analytical side understood the government's position, because cannabis was still a federally banned substance. Whether I wanted to or not, I had become the face of the medical-cannabis industry, and the federal government was watching my notoriety rise.

People close to me would ask, "Vince, aren't you scared they are going to come in and raid your dispensary and cart you off to a federal penitentiary?" My feeling was, *What are they going to achieve by doing that?* It felt like I was ahead of my time with the invention and all the publicity, but I was already at the point of no return and had to see things through. I had heard that being an entrepreneur is like jumping off a cliff with no parachute and building a plane on the way down. To me, this situation was no different except I was dealing with a Goliath in the DEA that could potentially crush me if it saw me as a menace of some sort.

We had just started building our client base at the dispensary, and we were following the right protocol. We weren't using unethical marketing techniques. Doctors recommended the medicine to patients if they felt it would offer relief from what ailed them. And we were thorough in screening our patients. We went the extra mile to verify that patients had valid documentation and would not accept anyone under twenty-one, the federal age of majority. Even if someone younger could legally possess and use the drug under state law, under federal law, he or she was still a minor. I always cautioned dispensary operators to handle things similarly for their own safety.

Other local dispensaries looked the other way and had heavier patient traffic to show for it. But it was more important to me to ensure all our i's were dotted and t's crossed at the dispensaries I briefly operated. We didn't arbitrarily stockpile medicine. We didn't do a high volume of cash transactions, and we certainly weren't selling pounds of cannabis out the back door that would ultimately be diverted to nonmedical users through street dealers. Everything was sold in small quantities for medicinal use to qualified patients. (I routinely told people that if anyone was smoking more than an ounce of cannabis every week or two, the odds were, *they* weren't smoking it but selling it on the street to nonmedical users.) I often said to concerned family and friends, "What's the worst that can happen? They come in and see this facility operated in the best possible manner." I would soon find out.

Meanwhile, to stay afloat financially, I decided to sell my Porsche for $50,000. The buyer was an older gentleman. He gave me his credit-card information and authorized a charge of $10,000 as a deposit. Then he told me he was leaving town for a couple of weeks on vacation and would be in touch while he was away to make further payment arrangements. He said he planned to pay the remaining $40,000 in two installments.

I never heard from the buyer during the time frame he told me he'd call, and I couldn't reach him after many tries. So I e-mailed him and said if I didn't hear from him by a certain date, I was going to charge his card for the balance. When I still didn't hear from him, I did what I had warned. When he got back from vacation, he was very upset that I'd charged the card without his permission. I showed him the e-mail and said, "This is not bad faith at all! Here are the e-mails I sent you…and here's what happened. You shouldn't be upset!" The matter escalated. In retrospect, I can see I should have taken better care of him to address the grievance he had with me.

There was a lot going on in my life at the time, and I was not as vigilant as I should have been. A note to other entrepreneurs: things can get twisted and misconstrued in the course of business transactions. Sometimes it's best not to go ahead with certain deals and to cancel pending transactions. Make amends after the fact with an aggrieved party, even if you think you are in the right. Sometimes conflicting personalities make transactions unworkable, and you may disagree with others over even concrete facts. Handle what needs to be handled, and focus on the next deal. Don't take it personally, and don't let it linger either. Come to terms with the aggrieved party. Sometimes a lawsuit isn't the worst possible outcome in a business dispute. Something far worse could be looming on the horizon.

The buyer went to the Department of Motor Vehicles (DMV), spoke to an investigator named George, and discovered my prior offense from when I was eighteen. After more investigation, he uncovered that I had made worldwide news concerning my invention. Later, I surmised that the local DMV investigator, George, looking to make a name for himself, had called the local DEA branch to stir something up.

So, one fine day in April of 2008, about two months after my mother's suicide, when Tom's firm was winding down and I was battling health issues from the mold-infested house that I would soon lose to foreclosure, I woke up to the California DMV Special Investigations Division, in concert with agents from the DEA, at my door at six thirty in the morning. They pounded hard for about five seconds and proceeded to ram the door. I hopped to my feet and rushed downstairs to find about ten agents who seemed ready to take on a militia.

To this day, I'm not clear on what they thought they would find at my residence, but what they found was me, a miniature pinscher dog, and a miniature longhaired dachshund. Fortunately, my girlfriend at the time was on a getaway to Miami Beach with friends, so she didn't have to deal with the absolute panic that ensued. I had about five semiautomatic guns pointed at my head, and I was in sleepwear and slippers. It was the most bizarre experience of my life to that point.

It was seven o'clock when they took me into custody. When my two dispensaries opened for business at eleven, DEA agents raided both. They took the managers into custody and questioned them about me. Prior to the raid, my thinking had been, *What are they going to do? I'm not doing anything wrong.* These dispensaries were tightly run, not-for-profit establishments. Between salaries, wages, keeping medicine on the shelves, and paying the rent, we were barely making enough to keep the doors open. I paid myself a modest management salary of about $3,000 per month for the time, effort, and energy necessary to operate a business like that. That was and still is the model for entrepreneurs in this industry, who conduct business in medical-cannabis states (as opposed to recreational-cannabis states that run as for-profit businesses, which came years later).

With that being said, we weren't like some dispensaries that had two or three hundred patients coming in each day. We barely had fifteen or twenty. I knew that to grow a business like that the right way, I needed to treat it as a medical clinic—not a pot shop. A lot of the competition treated their dispensaries as pot shops. I didn't advertise or market the dispensaries near high schools like some others were doing. Ours was a different type of establishment. We didn't cater to a younger clientele. We served a client base composed primarily of professionals—doctors, lawyers, even a Los Angeles Superior Court judge, who commented that he preferred our location as it was near his home and had a "professional look and feel" to it.

After DEA agents had questioned me for three hours, the DMV gumshoe, George, said, "You know, we brought a dog in to sniff around your house, and all we can figure is that you must have had enough time to flush the stuff down the toilet." That's when I realized that George had leveraged the whole case around the drug element to get the DEA interested. However, there were no illegal drugs to find! When they raided the dispensaries, they found all the proper documentation. They knocked holes in the walls, seemingly looking for weapons, heroin, opium, cocaine, methamphetamine, unreported cash, and pounds of cannabis—but there was nothing.

Moreover, interviews with my employees turned up nothing of substance, as everyone who worked for me knew I was all about running an honest and ethical medical dispensary. Both managers later told me that the questions had been pretty far out in left field. One manager recalls that George (of all people) had asked if I commonly returned on my private jet with pounds of opium from Iran. The manager had replied, "A, Vince doesn't have a private jet; B, Vince doesn't sell illegal drugs; and C, Vince is a good guy." I found out later that the criminal complaint filed against me had alleged that I owned a private jet and flew to exotic destinations to transport drugs.

Unfortunately, low-level investigators, who are trying to persuade district attorneys to file criminal complaints, commonly misrepresent facts to get their attention. Otherwise, the district attorney (DA) might pass on prosecuting the case the investigator hopes will get him or her promoted. One of my attorneys later told me that George was eventually fired for embellishing alleged facts on other cases as well.

In addition to confiscating our equipment and all the medication, the DEA froze all my bank accounts and seized a car from my house, which I later filed paperwork to reclaim. After studying the security footage from the dispensaries and dissecting every single financial record I had, they concluded that I wasn't using the dispensaries as a front for other illicit activities. This used to be a common suspicion from outsiders looking into the cannabis industry.

The DEA let me go without charging me with a crime. After the dust settled, it had found nothing to hang its hat on. In my mind, I rationalized that the DEA had discovered it wasn't dealing with a criminal after it and every other three-letter agency in the States, from the IRS to the FBI, had presumably looked into me. In the end, they probably just saw an overzealous kid in over his head (I was twenty-eight years old at the time). Even with that horrible experience, I have never held a poor opinion of our government and never will. I realize that the US government and all its different agencies, divisions, departments, all the way up to the White House, are simply doing the best they can in all phases. I do love this country very much and have always tried to be a positive influence in whatever I do.

After all had been said and done, the raids on my two dispensaries led to the improvement of my future inventions and refocusing of the business models years later. If it hadn't been for that incident, my future businesses might never have developed into the winners they ended up becoming. In hindsight, the raids turned out to be blessings in disguise. At the time, though, I was so dejected over the whole situation, I didn't even bother to file the paperwork to get the DEA to return my prototype machine. I could have gotten it back by filing an asset-forfeiture relief claim, as I did with the vehicle that had been seized, but I was done with the dispensing-machine project for the time being.

George at the DMV put together a four-count felony case against me based on the transaction with the car buyer. The allegations regarded one unauthorized charge on a credit card, simply pled four different ways. So, after eighteen months of going back and forth to court and ultimately just buying the car back, the prosecution on my case finally hit a dead end. The prosecutors agreed to give me community service, nail me on using a credit card without permission, and dismiss the other three counts. Unfortunately, the conviction appears as a credit-card fraud offense, which is unfortunate, because it implies that I was stealing strangers' identities or something similarly devious and morally repugnant. My attorney counseled me, "Take the damn deal and be done with it. This is an absolute victory!"

I didn't know at that point that I'd ever be an officer, director, and founder of a public company. If I could have seen into the future, I would have fought the charge at trial. But at the time, I thought, *So if, after two years, they've finally given up on prosecuting me, fine.* I now had two felonies on my record but hadn't served a day in jail for any of it. I know in my heart I'm not a bad person or a criminal, so who cares what's on my record? I control my own destiny, and I won't be defined by a rap sheet that means nothing in the grand scheme of things. At the time, it felt like I had narrowly escaped being a casualty of the system. I had put myself in certain situations and paid the price for it. However, I had a renewed energy, and I felt confident I could make my life work. The matter was resolved in August of 2009, well before I began operating what would later become Medbox Inc.

While I was still going back and forth to court, at every hearing, I kept seeing this strange-looking man, who always glared at me. At one of my final appearances on that case, I looked at my attorney and said, "See that guy?"

My lawyer said, "Yeah. What's the story with him?"

I said I had no idea but that he kept showing up at all my court appearances. Neither one of us thought it could be merely a coincidence.

My lawyer went up to him and said, "My client says you've been following him around. What's your interest in my client?" Instead of answering, the guy got up and walked out. Weeks later, this person appeared at my final hearing and was visibly upset when the judge dismissed the charges. He stormed out of the courtroom and made a scene as he walked out. It was very odd behavior. All I remember is looking at my attorney and both of us smiling awkwardly as if to ask, "What the hell was that about?"

I later discovered that the man was Joe, Los Angeles's consumer-affairs agent, conducting an investigation of Tom's law office. We wouldn't cross paths again until about a year later.

CHAPTER 6

—— ❧ ——

Tossed from the Frying Pan into the Fire

Questioning a man's character can empower him to
prove you wrong.

AFTER THE CLOSURE of Tom's law office, I reflected on my talents and considered ways I might use all the experience I had gathered over the years. That's when I came up with the idea to do consulting work for anyone looking to operate medical-cannabis dispensaries in Los Angeles and throughout California. By this time, medical cannabis had become a booming industry with plenty of people who wanted to get involved. During my six months of running these businesses, I had learned a lot—how to get permits and file and process the right incorporation paperwork, all while gaining invaluable hands-on management experience. I had also discovered how to run those businesses more efficiently and effectively through technology. The industry sorely needed that.

When I had sold my interest in the two dispensaries, I knew someday that the sentiment on the whole industry would change. When it did, I would revisit my project. With the election of Obama, government attitudes would eventually shift.

After I'd sent out retirement letters on Tom's behalf and turned my attention to consulting work, I received a letter from Joe with the Los Angeles Department of Consumer Affairs (DCA). However, this agent had first reached out to Tom while the law office was still running. The first letter Tom received had stated that a couple of clients had complained that their cases were not being properly handled. Tom had responded in writing to dispute the allegations and had attached case documents to show they had been handled properly up until his retirement. Joe also sent a letter to me, and I responded to the claims. A couple of letters went back and forth, and Tom had told me that he considered the matter closed.

When the law office shut down, I also considered the matter with the consumer-affairs agent to be closed. But the department had received a couple more complaints, as did the state bar, and so Joe reached out to me again via a forwarding address. According to this letter, the agent had a bone to pick with Tom, but Tom had failed to take the additional responsibility. At that point, the DCA had started to actively work up a case. From what I understand, Joe approached the district attorney a couple of times, but due to Tom's involvement as the attorney of record on the relevant cases, the DA's office declined to file a case. Since the issue involved an attorney's office that had gone under, the DA considered it a civil case rather than a criminal one.

Two years later, this issue with Joe and the DCA resurfaced. By then, I was running my private company, consulting for medical-cannabis-dispensary owners. I was helping them to get the necessary permits, form their corporations, and build out their storefronts. When dispensary owners wanted to sell their businesses, which was fairly frequently in Los Angeles, matching buyers with sellers became part of my consulting business. I matched entrepreneurs with opportunities, whether erecting new dispensaries and teaching the owners how to operate the business compliantly or introducing them to operating businesses with principals who wanted out for one reason or another.

One such entrepreneur was Abdul, a Pakistani who was intent on making a splash in the cannabis industry. His appetite was overly aggressive, and that should have been a warning sign for me that he was not a good candidate for placement. At the time, though, I was willing to help anyone who didn't have drug-related prior offenses gain entry. Abdul passed that test, so I began consulting for him. I then introduced him to several existing dispensaries that were on the market, as he wanted an already-established patient base.

His sights were set on a dispensary for sale in Canoga Park, California, which was being advertised as having a lot of patients and a positive cash-flow. I had a good relationship with the dispensary owner, JT, and became his sale intermediary. Ultimately, JT instructed me to accept a deposit of $50,000 from Abdul for the transfer of the business, with $300,000 more due. Unbeknown to me, JT had also accepted someone else's deposit within days of Abdul's.

JT sold to the other party, and I was left having to explain the situation to Abdul, who was upset and distraught over it. He even went to the dispensary to confront JT, who confirmed what had happened. I e-mailed Abdul, stating that he could have his deposit back or apply it toward another dispensary that I had available, one that he had already toured. I had entered into a purchase contract for it a few weeks prior, planning to flip it to a new owner without ever operating it. The escrow period on it was thirty days to close, and I was convinced that the market was hot enough that this would not put me at risk and I could transfer the business quickly at a profit. I had no tolerance for running a business like that while I was focused on developing my consulting business.

Abdul e-mailed that he would like to apply the deposit to this other dispensary. I had a lot of other interested parties but chose him since he was distraught over missing out on the first one. I completed my own purchase for $100,000 and immediately passed possession to Abdul for $300,000, with a contract that applied Abdul's deposit toward the price. I sourced new employees for Abdul, renovated the interior, and installed a new security system because he had complained that the current one was obsolete. I even prepaid for a whole year of liability insurance as an extra perk for Abdul.

After about three weeks, Abdul complained that the patient count was lower than he had expected and said that he wanted my consulting on marketing. I then contributed $5,000 toward a marketing campaign and showed him how to market the business in industry periodicals as well as online promotion to patients. Abdul seemed content, but that unfortunately didn't last for long. Four months later, he engaged an attorney by the name of Stanley. Stanley was openly hostile in a letter he wrote to me and demanded all monies be returned to Abdul. He said that his client no longer wanted to operate the business. I told him that this would be impossible, given that Abdul had been operating for months and had received continued consulting support from me during that time. The whole premise was ridiculous. The contract certainly didn't contain any language for a return allowance.

Months later, the demands became more and more unreasonable. Now Abdul wanted to keep the business but still receive a full refund. His attorney was claiming fraud. This claim came after they had discovered my two felonies, which seemed to give Abdul and Stanley the impression that they could have their way with me and make whatever weird and unusual demands they could conjure. I was unwavering in my position. I told them that they were being unreasonable and I would not entertain any of their outlandish demands.

A couple of months later, in February of 2010, I received a notice from the bank that the consulting company's business account had been debited for $300,000, due to a fraud claim tendered by Abdul and his attorney, Stanley. I was absolutely irate that the bank hadn't even asked my company for supporting paperwork. I immediately called and spoke to a representative, who was surprised that there was even a contract executed by Abdul, since the matter had been submitted to them as "check fraud." After we pieced it all together over the next few days, it became clear to the bank that Abdul had lied in his claim and that no "check fraud" had occurred. The funds were placed back into my company's business account, where they rightly belonged. The matter concluded with Abdul and Stanley sending me disparaging e-mails saying that they would "have the last laugh."

About a month later, I received a call from a detective with the Los Angeles Police Department (LAPD). She introduced herself and stated that Abdul had filed a criminal complaint against me for stealing money from him. I was again taken by surprise, but given the prior ordeal with the bank, I was prepared with documents, e-mails, and also a false affidavit that Abdul had provided to the bank that proved that Abdul was committing fraud—not me. The detective reviewed the materials and, after a few weeks, called me to let me know that the file was closed and the police wouldn't be looking into the matter further.

Two months later, I received a lawsuit from Abdul and Stanley. Adding insult to injury, they named my father as a codefendant. This was simply harassment. The only time Abdul had met my father was once in passing at my consulting business's office. The claim was that my father had told Abdul that the business he was buying was "a good business." My father never spoke to Abdul about anything business related. The only reason they had met was that my father used my office to maintain what was left of his insurance practice. While I met with Abdul to finalize paperwork on the dispensary purchase, my father headed home for the day and simply said good-bye to me. I introduced Abdul to my father, and that was their entire interaction—a "nice to meet you" and a handshake.

My father was not a consultant or an officer or an employee of my company. He was not a signer on any of my business accounts. He had nothing to do with anything related to my business pursuits and hadn't since the closure of the legal and referral businesses in 2008. The facts don't matter to characters like Abdul and Stanley. They just wanted to harass and oppress, especially after I had beat them at their own game with the bank and later the LAPD.

My consulting business would soon be rebranded as Medbox, which combined industry consulting with the dispensing machine I had invented. I packaged the machine in a comprehensive and turnkey consulting bundle for entrepreneurs, with increased oversight and transparency. Prior to 2010, my consulting practice had not involved any machine sales. The new version was a start-up, and although business was good, I was only receiving a few thousand dollars in salary per month, so the lawsuit was a bit of a scare for me. I didn't know how I was going to afford a good attorney.

I had a deep understanding of how these cases could play out, and even though I knew I would prevail, it might cost me hundreds of thousands of dollars and several years to fight the case prior to a trial on the merits. I was at a loss until I actually met with an attorney. He looked at my $2.1 million state and federal tax liens from 2003 through 2007 that I had signed off on with the IRS, and he recommended I file bankruptcy. He advised that this could resolve the tax debt and also get the Abdul lawsuit dismissed. I was elated at the possibilities. I did file for personal bankruptcy, and because my father had also been named in the suit and I was basically supporting him, he filed as well.

This move stayed (paused) Abdul's lawsuit until the bankruptcy court could discharge (finalize) the bankruptcy. Abdul and Stanley filed an adversary proceeding with the bankruptcy court that claimed fraud and brought up my "criminal history." The purpose of an adversary proceeding is for a creditor, which Abdul was posing as, to demonstrate that the defendants seeking bankruptcy protection had committed elements of fraud and therefore did not deserve it. At the hearing on the matter, the bankruptcy judge ruled that no fraud had occurred. Abdul and Stanley had once again lost, and this was the death knell for their purported claims against my father and me. The court formally discharged the bankruptcy shortly thereafter, and I figured that our dealings with Abdul and his attorney, Stanley, were over.

About three months later, on October 28, 2010, I parked my car at work and was about to head upstairs to my office when the sheriff's department arrested me in the parking lot. An odd-looking, portly man waddled toward me as if he, himself, were a police officer. It was Joe— the mystery man who had showed up at the hearings during my previous court case. He looked at me and said, "Now I've got you!"

The police took me upstairs and also arrested my father, specifically to put pressure on me. My arrest culminated in fifteen felony criminal counts, while my father was charged with three misdemeanors. All of these charges were relative to cases that my father's attorney-referral service had referred to Tom's law office.

The charges made no sense. My father had been operating a licensed lawyer-referral service, and I had been an employee of an attorney. There had been nothing untoward about what we were doing. But they were holding me financially responsible for all the money that clients had pre-paid to Tom and we could not reimburse. The clients' retainers had already gone toward the operation of the law office and to Tom himself, so there was no money to recoup. It's not like we had squirreled money away somewhere in hidden assets or in other people's names, which would have been easy to track for investigators. It simply had not occurred.

The prosecution was determined to get someone to repay the clients, but Tom himself had no assets, and if they charged him, he would have an absolute defense that would also have protected me. So instead, they charged me and added my father so they could sell a story to the DA that I had been operating a law office without an attorney and that my father knew it, referring cases anyway. It made no difference to them that I wasn't the one who had received the clients' monies or that the clients had retained Tom with it. It also made no difference that my father had been operating a perfectly legal and licensed service. None of those facts mattered to Joe, who was grinning and smiling at me during the entire arrest. What mattered was that my father and I were in handcuffs in broad daylight, for all to see.

We were sent to Los Angeles County jail. This was my father's first time in jail, at seventy-five years old. When I had been taken into custody before, I had been released the same day. Not this time. A father and son being in jail together is a horrible thing, and for the first three days, I couldn't eat. I was very depressed. Meanwhile, I still had to keep my consulting service going. I gave my assistant instructions on how to deal with the clients in my absence—what he should and shouldn't do or say. My consulting and machine-selling business was still relatively new, and my clients needed attention. It was very difficult to be powerless, unable to affect my own destiny.

About four days in, I figured out a way to bail my father out. He was obviously my first priority. His bail had been set at $50,000, so I made a few calls to friends, one of whom put up their house as collateral and paid a bail premium, and my father was a free man again. But I was stuck; my bail was half a million dollars. The way the arrest report was written, I had been painted as a high-rolling, faux lawyer conducting my supposed nefarious activities and defrauding all who crossed my path.

They told me I couldn't use any of my own assets to bail myself out, and they froze the business accounts from my new venture (that later became Medbox) and all my personal accounts. Their assertion was that anything in which I was involved had to be a criminal enterprise. They froze everything. They were essentially saying to me, "Go ahead and bail yourself out, but you can't use any of your money or the money of any of the relatives who get money from you." They considered everything tainted. Those in charge of prosecuting the case, in concert with Joe and the DCA, figured that if they put pressure on me, I'd just give up and die in jail. That would have been a win-win for them, because they wouldn't have had to prove their case at trial. Meanwhile, my father began trying to locate friends and family who were financially unaffiliated with me on any level to see if they'd be willing to put up their property as collateral to get me out.

While I was locked up, I was forced to make do and find common ground with my cellmates. Thankfully, I know how to get along with all types, so I became the resident know-it-all on legal matters, given my experience at managing law firms. Anyone who had problems with their cases came to me for some free advice. Although I told them I wasn't an attorney, I did have valuable knowledge on every type of case imaginable, from custody disputes to civil matters to federal-appellate motions. I had seen and done it all for clients of the firms I had worked at for eight years. That's what kept me safe. Joe, who had been gunning for me for a while, probably thought I'd get manhandled in there and die. He expected me to get beaten up and tortured. He underestimated me.

During the first thirteen days in jail, I'd only been to court once. Meanwhile, I had to sit by and watch my consulting business slide into a more and more precarious position in my absence. I had just started getting traction with the new venture, and now it would soon be in sham-bles. My consulting clients needed attention, and I wasn't there. I was dealing with my assistant by phone, trying to keep my business alive. Thankfully I was in "general population," a prison-dorm-type situation, with phone privileges. My assistant tried to keep things afloat, but he was getting more and more flustered because situations kept arising that he didn't know how to handle. At that point, I realized, *If I don't get out of here, my business will be completely gone...everything I've worked for will go down the drain.*

My father was having a hard time finding someone with enough eq-uity to post property as collateral. Just in case, I'd removed a blade from a razor that the prison provided to inmates, and I'd hidden it in my cot. Security didn't make daily checks of our personal belongings, so only an-other inmate would potentially have found it. If things didn't turn around by the next day, I had my plan in place to end it all.

The following morning, I got up and started getting ready to go to court. This was the day that would decide my fate. Either my father would come through with someone to bail me out, or I had that razor blade ready. Sitting in jail, beginning to lose hope that I would ever be bailed out, I thought about the case against me. When the DA's office had filed the case, they were trying to establish me as a Madoff-type character based on the assertions of Joe and the DCA. They had charged me with fifteen felonies, considering each client separately. They claimed I had stolen from every single one and absconded with the money. They had neglected to mention that all these clients had signed contracts with a licensed attorney and that they had paid the attorney—*not me*! In fact, they failed to mention Tom, the attorney, at all. They had said, in essence, that I was a serial sociopath, taking advan-tage of people left and right!

The prosecution's job was to make the case seem as egregious as possible, but at the end of the day, they had the burden of proving it. The DCA knew that Tom was the responsible party. But, after repeat-edly bringing the story to the DA's office that repeatedly declined to prosecute, the agency had decided to change the facts of the case. This left the DA's office no choice but to file.

As I read the criminal complaint against me in greater detail, I noticed something strange. Abdul was listed as one of the people I had allegedly defrauded with Tom's office. That didn't make any sense at all, since the transaction with Abdul had happened years after Tom's office had closed its doors. How could this be? Then it dawned on me that Abdul and Stanley, after I had handed them defeat after defeat through the bank, the LAPD, and the court system, had finally found someone who would give them credence, ignoring the true facts and the documents that verified them. They found Joe.

When Abdul and Stanley interfaced with Joe, my destiny took an odd turn. Together, they had manufactured the missing piece of the puzzle that would finally get the DA's office interested in filing a case against me. The dollar figure would have been too low at first, with each of the fourteen law-office clients paying between $1,000 and $5,000. That only amounted to a little over $60,000. In addition, some of those clients had already been reimbursed with whatever funds the firm had left in the operating accounts or by the state bar directly, bringing the amount even lower. However, with Abdul and his $300,000 theft claim, that tipped the scales into another category altogether, making the case more appealing to the DA. So they threw Abdul's claim and law-office clients from Tom's office into one case. Still, to this day, I can't even fathom how they could draw a link between the two, but I guess where there's a will there's a way.

I realized all this as I was in jail on my thirteenth day, awaiting news of whether or not I'd make bail. This day would be a turning point in my life, one way or another. If my father was unable to find someone outside the family with assets they could use to bail me out, all was lost. There would be nothing to come back to. I knew my business wouldn't survive me being stuck in jail while having to defend myself at trial. Suicidal thoughts crept back into my consciousness, and it became more and more of a possibility with every minute that passed. Then my fear turned into something else, and I started to have faith that things would turn around. I turned my rage into resolve, my fear into faith, and my lemons into lemonade. I was ready to take on the world again.

As I dressed for court that morning, I was acutely aware of the razor blade hidden among my personal effects. I took a stroll over to the common-area bathroom, packed the blade into a paper towel, and threw it away. My mother had taken that way out, and it scarred her family forever. I was not going to let life get the best of me. Plus, I had forgotten something very important: I had a guardian angel looking after me. That was my ace in the hole, not some stupid razor blade.

I appeared that morning in court, and, to my surprise, my father had pulled off a miracle. At the eleventh hour, a friend of my father's, who'd known me as a child, saved the day. He owned a retail establishment in Beverly Hills where he sold sunglasses, and he had put it up as collateral to bail me out. I was released from jail that very morning. No one ever knew how close I had come to taking my own life. Then again, I met my demons head on and prevailed. It was cathartic! I felt healed. On top of it, I checked the business accounts upon my release. The DA's office had missed an account that had over $100,000 in it. That $100,000 was all I needed to resurrect and maintain my company after my two-week hiatus and the freezing of funds in other accounts. My guardian angel was hard at work, pushing the scales of justice in my favor.

As a condition of my release on bail, I had to wear an ankle monitor. There was no set time for the monitor to be removed; the obligation was open-ended. After all, the criminal complaint had painted me as a high roller who might fly off to the south of France or somewhere at a moment's notice. The irony about the jet-setting lifestyle they purported was that it could be easily debunked by simply examining my passport, which showed I had only left the country once since childhood—a pleasure trip to Cabo San Lucas, Mexico. I had had no time to travel. I was busy all those years, working seventy-hour workweeks and supporting my parents!

The case against me continued for about three years while Joe and his DCA cohorts poked around in my business affairs and actively solicited clients I had done consulting business with to file claims against me. That only resulted in the former clients contacting me to report this and tell me that they had no grievances with me whatsoever. In the first year, I had to be home every evening at a set time, or the ankle monitor would alert law enforcement to throw me back in jail. Life didn't stop just because I was wearing the monitor. I still had to run my business and look after my clients, some of whom were located in Arizona.

By late 2011, the company was booming with activity, and we began the transition to going public. I rebranded the company as Medbox. We had achieved a lot of success in 2010 and 2011, by setting up dozens of dispensaries throughout California and also by getting an unprecedented number of coveted dispensary-business licenses for our many clients in Arizona. The company was a breakout success! I did it all by myself, for the most part, all while having a fifteen-felony-count indictment pending in Los Angeles criminal court.

There were times I had to hop an early-morning flight to Arizona, take care of my business there, catch a return flight, and be back in my apartment before ten at night. God forbid I should run into traffic or any delays. There was no wiggle room. I had to be home on time or appear before a judge to explain myself. That scenario wouldn't have been pleasant.

CHAPTER 7

— ✄ —

Fifteen Felony Counts...and a
Publicly Traded Company

<u>Intense pressure can turn a piece of coal into a diamond.</u>

I WAS LIVING under a microscope in every phase of my life. The ankle monitor stayed on at all times—even in the shower. As far as I could tell, its main purpose was to make its wearer feel subhuman—like an enemy of the state. It stripped me of my confidence and constantly reminded me of my case. When you're wearing a bracelet around your ankle, you can't forget for a minute. It was always on my mind, exactly as intended. The criminal-justice system makes a person feel demoralized. The DCA had presented me as an absolute swindler, a shyster. I was public enemy number one in their eyes, and they wanted to make sure I was sufficiently pacified.

My case went on for another two years after the removal of the ankle monitor. I had to go to court every couple of months, and even though I knew I was innocent of the charges, the case weighed on me. Like everyone else in such a position, I wanted to believe that my attorneys were unequivocally on my side. But I had spent enough time in law offices to know that wasn't necessarily true. Lawyers are often jaded and actually disinclined to give people the benefit of the doubt. Most have heard and seen it all, so they feel like they know it all. They have a hard time digesting anything outside their comfort zone.

In my case, all the lawyers could see was a young man charged with fifteen felony counts. My own attorneys at first operated under the mistaken impression that Tom had been incapacitated in a hospital some-where while I practiced illegally using his law license. But Tom had been healthy enough in his fifties and a very active participant in the office. Though he preferred to send associate attorneys to make court appear-ances instead of going himself, he did appear in court on occasion.

To substantiate my defense, I spent four weeks and an estimated eighty hours assembling the executed retainer agreements between Tom and the fourteen clients, checks paid to Tom, e-mails to and from the cli-ents regarding work on their cases, and claims submitted to the state bar in which each of the clients admitted that Tom was their attorney and any grievance was with him and not me, as well as definitive evidence con-cerning the Abdul matter. The summary I prepared, along with labeled attachments, resulted in a five-inch-thick, three-ring binder stuffed with almost nine hundred pages of evidence.

I reproduced the records for my team of three attorneys, each of whom possessed talents that I felt blended well together. I had to carry the binders in one of those rolling suitcases—each one weighed about fifteen pounds. My attorneys were absolutely shocked that I had pre-pared such a comprehensive defense. One marveled, "I wish all my cli-ents did this."

I said, "Well, as much as I did it for you, I actually did it for myself! I need to get you prepared because I will not accept prison time and I will not accept a plea deal. I am ready to go to trial." Within days of that encounter with my defense team, I paid the fees for the three of them to take the case all the way to trial. I even retained an expert-witness attorney who specialized in attorney ethics and business practices. My attorneys already knew I was smart, but after seeing my binders and my forward thinking in retaining an expert to testify at trial, they looked at me through different eyes.

I then organized for all the paralegals and attorneys who had worked in Tom's office to meet with my defense so they could corroborate my facts. After my attorneys reviewed my binder and interviewed the witnesses, they were all on my side and were determined to get the case resolved favorably for me.

Despite the intense scrutiny and pressure under which I was living my life, I somehow managed to hang on to my sense of self. I was determined to turn the pressure into something miraculous—to turn the lump of coal in my Christmas stocking into a diamond. I take great pride in the fact that I did not crack under such scrutiny. I was not going to let the state make me feel like a menace to society when I knew I was not.

I didn't want to succumb to the pressure, have a nervous breakdown, and be seen as a failure or a cautionary tale. I knew that Joe, Abdul, and Stanley would enjoy that too much. I set out to overcome all the obstacles standing in my way and prove not just that I wasn't a criminal, but that I was also a special type of entrepreneur—one that would inspire others to achieve and overcome even the most insurmountable of obstacles. I knew that once I was through my ordeals, I would write about them, but at the time, I simply forced myself to live each day as it came and never allowed myself to think too far ahead. The possibility of somehow not prevailing at trial was all too real. So many others had been convicted of crimes they hadn't committed, so I felt no real solace in knowing I was innocent. Innocence is in the eye of the beholder, and perception dominates reality at times in the world we live in.

I was dealing with many clients in my current business. If I had had a nervous breakdown and let it fail, those clients would have been left high and dry and not taken care of. They wouldn't have received what my company had promised. The work I had promised them would have been left unfinished, mirroring what had happened when Tom retired. But in this case, I would have been the one responsible. There would have been no one I could point to and say, "No, it wasn't me; it was him!" It truly would have been me. That's what kept me going—the knowledge that if things were under my control, I had to make sure I performed in the right way. Had I given up, a Madoffesque scandal *would* have ensued, confirming the suspicions of the DCA. I didn't want to give all my detractors the satisfaction, and I didn't want to let down the people who trusted and believed in me.

If I possess a secret ingredient, an essential trait that separates me from those who cash in their chips and call it a day to the detriment of others, it's this: the desire to do the best I can for those who believe in me, combined with the will to prove my detractors wrong. This character trait drives a lot of people to greatness. Being confronted by doubters and wanting to prove them wrong can be a powerful, motivating force.

While I was persistent with my attorneys about getting the case resolved, the prosecution kept postponing the trial date. Finally, I told my lawyers that I was done with it and pushed for immediate resolution. It was January of 2013, nearly thirty months from the date I was first charged. My company, Medbox, now a publicly traded company of which I was the majority shareholder, had reached epic proportions on Wall Street, and I was worth over a whopping billion dollars at that point. I needed the case resolved, because the last thing I wanted was for my detractors to find a way to sabotage my company—to the detriment of all the shareholders of Medbox, not just me.

I then realized that being even more proactive was my best bet. I swallowed my pride, and for the greater good, I reached out to Abdul and Stanley via e-mail and proposed that we resolve the dispute. I agreed to return all monies he had paid to me if he returned the business, thus placing us in our original positions prior to the transaction.

Of course, Abdul and Stanley had been keenly following my successes at Medbox. Abdul countered my offer, with him keeping the business plus a payback of $250,000—and the kicker; he wanted $100,000 worth of Medbox stock! A major impediment in business that all entrepreneurs need to resolve is ego, and if I accepted this deal, I would be checking my ego at the door for the greater good of the shareholders of Medbox and for myself, in resolving the claim of the major "victim" in the pending criminal case against me. Abdul had used every available avenue to make his claims against me, and I had prevailed every time. However, my freedom, the well-being of Medbox, and, most importantly, my father's health and mental state were enough to make me see the bigger picture and not allow ego or pride get in the way of sound decision-making.

I accepted the deal with Abdul with one caveat: he would sign a notarized statement that I had conducted myself appropriately in all my business dealings with him. Specifically, the language was as follows:

> WHEREAS, "Abdul" acknowledge that:
> Mehdizadeh had fulfilled all his responsibilities pertaining to the subject agreements between the parties, or if services had not been performed, Mehdizadeh was restricted from performance by "Abdul."

Abdul agreed with the language, and Stanley reviewed the settlement agreement and approved it. The statement meant nothing to a guy like Abdul, even though it directly contradicted everything he had told the DCA and DA's office. Abdul was all about the money. His greed resulted in him keeping the business I had sold him, me actually paying him more than a full refund for it, and $100,000 in Medbox stock as a bonus. I would have paid him double simply to see his notarized signature on a document stating that, for all intents and purposes, he had perjured himself in statements to law enforcement about his business dealings with me. Our agreement was good enough for me and reaffirmed my innocence of any wrongdoing in my business dealings with Abdul. Abdul had received a sweet deal from me simply because I had reached a level of wealth that less than 1 percent of the world's population would ever achieve. Abdul became a beneficiary of my success.

Shortly thereafter, I even received a warm e-mail from Abdul:

> Best of luck
> I remember when u told me about the PVM machine over three years ago. U are a smart sob after all.
> Good luck
> Abdul

I once again thought Abdul and Stanley were forever out of my life. However, greed causes people to lose their sense of self and dignity. Money corrupts those who have weak moral character. I didn't know it at the time, but Abdul and Stanley would attempt to extort hundreds of thousands of dollars of additional cash from me years later. They threatened to go back to the DA and file a new case on the same charges! I laughed and filed an extortion and harassment lawsuit against Abdul that is currently pending in Los Angeles Superior Court. People like Abdul and Stanley are bottom-feeders and don't know the definition of fair dealing or integrity. They are in a perpetual state of hatred for anyone who is doing better than they are.

I clued my attorneys in to what I was doing, but they were very wary of my contact with an alleged "victim" in the pending criminal matter. I made sure I blind copied each of them on every e-mail I sent to Abdul and Stanley so they could be privy to the interactions. When the next court date rolled around, the DA proposed a deal that involved six months in county jail. My response through my attorneys was, "We're going to trial!" From then on, the offers started getting better and better.

Then the prosecution presented a possible resolution. My attorneys explained that if I would plead guilty to two felonies, I wouldn't get any jail time. After a few years of probation, the felony convictions would be expunged. "Oh, and by the way," they added, "they want you to pay four hundred and fifty thousand dollars to the alleged victims, three hundred and fifty thousand of which you have already paid to Abdul of your own volition."

I weighed my decision. I had been fully prepared to take the case all the way to trial from the start. I felt certain that the evidence I had gathered would have proven my case. But I had my father to consider. He had been charged with the crime of referring cases to an illegally operating law office. The prosecution had targeted him as a means of leverage against me. Though this was all outrageous, my father was seventy-eight years old, and I decided not to put him through the rigors of a trial.

I also had to consider the impact to my business. My company would have been negatively affected by the public speculation that accompanies such trials. Had it not been for the negative impact upon my father's health and my business, I have no doubt that I would have prevailed at trial. So again, I made a decision for the greater good and accepted the plea deal, with the following caveat: I would enter a "West" plea on the two felony counts, meaning that I denied guilt but accepted the terms of the plea. The money was not an issue either since I had already paid most of the $450,000 months before. With that arrangement in place, the case was dismissed.

The DCA agent, Joe, was very agitated by the outcome of my case, but the fact remained that I was being charged with crimes I hadn't committed, and the DA's office just couldn't push the case any further. Joe had attended every hearing with the exception of the last three. After the DA offered me a no-jail-time deal, Joe resorted to e-mailing the prosecutors in the case to excite them about my successes in the public markets with Medbox.

One such e-mail that my attorneys made me privy to stated that I was engaged in "pump and dump" activity with Medbox. Obviously, Joe didn't understand what "pump and dump" was. I had not sold a single share of Medbox stock in 2011 or 2012, when he made the allegation; in fact, I didn't sell one in the public markets until the last quarter of 2013, when I was certain that Medbox's market was "real" and that the investors we had initially sold shares to had an opportunity to exit profitably before I, as the founder, received any benefit from my hard work in building the company.

My response to Joe was the following, sent in December of 2012, copied to my legal team as well as to a few of Joe's colleagues at DCA:

Mr. Joe XXXXX:
I was made privy to your email to the prosecutors on my pending matter whereas you made allegations that the recent overwhelming success and rise in share price of Medbox, Inc., the

company I work for, was in some way a "pump and dump" scenario. The insinuation that the company officers and/or affiliates are secretly liquidating the stock is unfounded and has no factual basis whatsoever. Fortunately for Medbox, Inc. and myself, none of the affiliates, including myself, have liquidated even one share of stock as all the company stock, besides that which is freely trading which no affiliates have any control over, is restricted from sale on the public markets. Any illegal transgressions would be on the SEC radar in a moments notice and easily uncovered through electronic transaction record keeping. This is especially true for a company in the spotlight, which Medbox is.

You seem to be the type that laments over others successes. Well, let me further put you on notice that the culmination of years of tireless work, dedication, solid financials, a patented invention that is relevant in today's marketplace in many different industries, along with a specific mention by the Wall Street Journal as to Medbox being a good investment, caused the share price to skyrocket more than 3000%. What you failed to mention in your email to prosecutors is that Medbox itself issued cautions to investors in press releases when the stock price seemed overinflated. Companies simply don't do that unless they are investor focused which Medbox absolutely is. Medbox does not even have an investor relations firm that promotes its stock because the company hasn't found a reputable enough firm to do so. All of the press attention, etc. happened organically and with good reason as Medbox is a viable and reputable company. In addition, the company is in the process of a financial audit performed by an independent auditing firm that will assist the company to its transition to fully reporting status within the 1st quarter of 2013. This audit accompanies a filing with the SEC where every aspect of the business will be scrutinized before being allowed to become an "SEC Fully

Reporting Company." While that level of scrutiny might make many people cringe, I welcome it. Building something from nothing is a joy not many people get to experience in their lifetimes.

I wish you and your family the best this holiday season. Maybe you will catch the hint and focus your attention on real criminals instead of wasting your time lobbying people against me. This email is not intended to start a dialogue and I will be blocking your communication from this point on.

Regards,

Vincent Mehdizadeh

A few months later, the case against me was formally dismissed at a final court hearing, through a plea agreement with the DA's office. One thing I hadn't been familiar with was the necessity for local government agencies to promote the conclusion of cases. To my surprise, the DA's office put out the following press release days after the resolution of my criminal matter:

LOS ANGELES COUNTY DISTRICT ATTORNEY'S OFFICE

Father, Son Plead to Criminal Charges in $450,000 Unauthorized Practice of Law Case

A father and son accused of stealing $450,000 from more than a dozen victims by offering unlicensed legal services pleaded no contest today, the Los Angeles County District Attorney's Office announced.

Pejman Mehdizadeh, 35, of Los Angeles, told victims he was a licensed attorney or that he worked with one and that he could provide a variety of services—including obtaining green cards, loan modifications and divorces. His father, Parvis Mehdizadeh,

78, of Calabasas, assisted. Between 2002 and 2009, they took payments from 15 victims ranging from $2,000 to $200,000.

"The District Attorney's Office is deeply committed to prosecuting cases of unauthorized practice of law and immigration fraud," said Los Angeles County District Attorney Jackie Lacey. She applauded the meticulous work of Deputy District Attorneys Kathleen Tuttle of the Consumer Protection Division and Dana Aratani who prosecuted the case. The younger Mehdizadeh pleaded no contest to two counts of felony grand theft and admitted a special allegation of engaging in a pattern of related felony conduct involving takings in excess of $100,000. Los Angeles County Superior Court Judge Robert J. Perry immediately sentenced him to four years in state prison, suspended, and five years of formal probation.

Under the terms of a negotiated plea agreement, the son was ordered to pay back $450,000 in restitution on or by Oct. 21 or face prison time. To date, he has paid $370,000 in restitution. The elder Mehdizadeh pleaded no contest to a misdemeanor violation of failure to obtain a bond required of those providing immigration assistance and was sentenced to three days in the county jail and two years of summary probation.

The case was investigated by the Los Angeles County District Attorney's Bureau of Investigations and the Los Angeles County Department of Consumer Affairs.

While I didn't agree with the summary offered by the DA's office, I was happy to have the case concluded and decided it wasn't worth the battle to have my attorneys reach out and demand recourse for the release. However, to add insult to injury, the DA's press release was followed by an even more defamatory one from the DCA:

COUNTY OF LOS ANGELES DEPARTMENT OF CONSUMER AFFAIRS NEWS ALERT—FOR IMMEDIATE RELEASE

Father-and-Son Team of Phony Immigration Consultants Convicted of Fraud, Must Pay Nearly One-Half Million Dollars in Restitution to Victims

LOS ANGELES—A father-and-son team who pretended to be a law firm and defrauded dozens of victims seeking immigration help have pled guilty to multiple charges of grand theft.

Brian J. Stiger, Director of the County of Los Angeles Department of Consumer Affairs (DCA), has announced today that Pejman Vincent Mehdizadeh and Parviz Paul Mehdizadeh were ordered to pay full restitution to victims who reported their losses to DCA.

The Mehdizadehs took money for immigration cases and either did not file or filed fraudulent documents with US Citizenship and Immigration Services (USCIS). They are responsible for defrauding victims out of hundreds of thousands of dollars while offering services in areas such as immigration, bankruptcy, divorce, and mortgage modifications, often without providing any services. Many of the Mehdizadehs' victims were forced to leave the country because of their failure to file appropriate documents.

Pejman Vincent Mehdizadeh, 34, of Los Angeles, pled to two felony grand theft counts and Parviz Paul Mehdizadeh, 78, of Calabasas, pled to one misdemeanor count.
Restitution will approach a half a million dollars, not including money distributed from the State Bar of California Restitution Fund, most of which has already been collected and distributed to the known victims.

"Immigration consultants often tell consumers that they have 'special connections' or know about secret programs to help immigrants become legal citizens," Director Stiger said. "They will say anything to gain your trust and take your money. Consumers should remember that if it sounds too good to be true, it probably is."

The Mehdizadehs also ran a lawyer referral service, under the name Active Lawyer Referral Service, and referred clients to themselves.

The prosecutors were Dana Aratani and Kathleen Tuttle of the Los Angeles County District Attorney's office.

I then took to the newswire myself and released this response in July 2013:

P. Vincent Mehdizadeh, a corporate executive, announced today that he has resolved a pending matter initiated by the Los Angeles County Department of Consumer Affairs from activities occurring from 2005–2008 relating to a law firm Mehdizadeh used to manage, as a non-attorney manager, alongside a supervising attorney, Thomas R. Lee.

"After three years of intense scrutiny into my personal and business life, the District Attorney's office finally gave up and conceded that I wasn't the person that they portrayed me to be," stated Mehdizadeh.

Thomas R. Lee, the attorney Mr. Mehdizadeh worked for, resigned from the practice of law with charges pending from the State Bar in 2008, for matters that predated his working relationship with Mr. Mehdizadeh. Mr. Lee closed his office abruptly— leaving clients without legal representation and angry that their cases were not completed as promised by Mr. Lee. In 2010, Mr. Mehdizadeh was formally charged for cases that were handled in that attorney's office from 2005–2008. Mr. Mehdizadeh explained, "That attorney, who has been disbarred since 2008, has no assets to speak of, so of course the person they target is the one who does. They wanted someone to pay the clients back and it made no difference to them that I wasn't the one who received the money from the clients as long as I had deep enough pockets to pay them."

Mr. Mehdizadeh accepted a plea arrangement whereas he entered a "West" Plea on 2 counts, meaning he denied guilt but accepted the terms of the plea. He was put on probation and volunteered payment to the victims of Mr. Lee's office. It was specifically negotiated that Mehdizadeh would qualify for an automatic expungement, or deletion, of the record after probation was successfully concluded.

Interestingly, while Mr. Lee was never charged with a crime, Mr. Mehdizadeh's own father was also charged with a crime for referring cases to the firm, while operating a properly permitted, state licensed, lawyer referral service.

"I was ready to take the case all the way as I had personally organized 843 pages of evidence that confirmed that the attorney I was working with received the funds from the aggrieved clients and not me. In addition, documents pulled from State Bar complaint records demonstrated that every single client admitted to hiring Mr. Lee and not me," stated Mehdizadeh. "However, with a 78 year old father being targeted as a means of leverage against me, I wasn't about to put him through a trial that we would have ultimately won, but possibly at a severe detriment to his health and mental well-being," he added. "Had his health not been an issue and the company I currently work for not been negatively affected by the speculation that accompanies such trials, I would have contested the matter and

prevailed. As it is, a payment was made voluntarily to law office clients from 2005–2008 from whom I did not retain funds, but the attorney did."

Mr. Mehdizadeh states that he has no ill will towards the prosecutors in the matter who conducted themselves professionally. His qualm was with how the case was presented to the prosecutors by the LA County Department of Consumer Affairs and specifically a field agent whom Mehdizadeh believes coerced testimony from Mr. Lee's clients in order to suit his agenda against Mehdizadeh.

"I am aware that calls were placed to individuals with whom I had business dealings by this particular consumer affairs agent and those people were told I was a 'bad guy' and to come file a complaint to get money back. I received a couple calls from people that stated as much and that they had no issue with me at all," stated Mehdizadeh. "It is a sad world we live in when people in positions of authority abuse that authority."

These three press releases demonstrate that perception and "spin" are all-important factors in today's world. The DA's office had its own agenda: claiming success in a wrongful suit that had cost the taxpayers of California hundreds of thousands of dollars. The DCA also had an agenda—to put my business career to an end because they were angry at the case's favorable outcome for me.

I'm a fighter by nature and have learned that if you don't push back when wronged, you will continue to be steamrolled your entire life. I took an offensive posture and hired an attorney immediately to claim defamation against the county of Los Angeles for what its Department of Consumer Affairs had written about me. The letter read as follows:

Dear Mr. Stiger:
This firm represents Pejman Vincent Mehdizadeh with respect to his claims against the Los Angeles County Department of

Consumer Affairs ("DCA"). This letter serves as a notice of governmental tort claims by Mr. Mehdizadeh against Los Angeles County and the DCA. Please direct any future correspondence regarding this matter to my attention.

On or about June 28, 2013, DCA issued a press release titled: "Father-and-Son Team of Phony Immigration Consultants Convicted of Fraud, Must Pay Nearly One-Half Million Dollars in Restitution to Victims." (Attached as Exhibit 1). This press release contains numerous factual inaccuracies that have the intention of defaming my client and causing tremendous injury to his reputation. Given the gross inaccuracies and choice of wording, it is apparent that the DCA either acted intentionally or, at a minimum, with a reckless disregard for the truth.

The numerous inaccuracies are described below:

1. The press release states that Mr. Mehdizadeh was convicted of "fraud." This assertion is false. In reality, he pled guilty to two counts of grand theft pursuant to Penal Code 186.11.

2. The press release inaccurately states that Mr. Mehdizadeh was a "phony immigration consultant." This statement is untrue. He was neither accused nor convicted of being a "phony" immigration consultant.

3. The press release states that Mr. Mehdizadeh, along with his father, "pretended to be a law firm." Mr. Mehdizadeh did not pretend to be a "law firm." This assertion is factually inaccurate. Instead, he managed the operations of a law firm and worked under the direction of a licensed attorney, who was the attorney of record for all of the cases at issue.

4. The press release states that Mr. Mehdizadeh was "ordered to pay full restitution to victims..." This statement is misplaced. Mr. Mehdizadeh, however, voluntarily compensated alleged victims, even though they were aggrieved by the attorney (and not Mr. Mehdizadeh).

5. The press release states that Mr. Mehdizadeh "filed fraudulent documents with the US Citizenship and Immigration Services (USCIS)." This assertion is categorically false. Mr. Mehdizadeh was neither accused nor convicted of filing fraudulent documents with the USCIS. In fact, if true, that would be within the exclusive jurisdiction of federal prosecutors, and not the Los Angeles District Attorney's Office.

6. The press release states: "Many of the Mehdizadehs' victims were forced to leave the country because of their failure to file appropriate documents." This statement is unsubstantiated and, in fact, was never proven.

As outlined above, there are numerous statements within the press release that are patently false. The severity or the inaccuracies demonstrate an intent to mislead readers and damage the reputation of Mr. Mehdizadeh. The DCA may seek to rely on the principle of sovereign immunity and, specifically, Cal. Civil Code Section 47. This assertion, however, is misplaced. The absolute immunity applies only when statements are made in the "proper discharge of an official duty." See McQuirk v. Donnelley, 189 F3d 793, 800 (9th Cir. 1999); Neary v. Regents of University of California, 185 Cal App. 3d 1136 (1986). In this instance, the Los Angeles County District Attorney's Office was likely acting within the scope of its official duty when it drafted a similar press release. The DCA, however, was not acting within the scope of its official duty because it had no authority to prosecute Mr. Mehdizadeh. Thus, the DCA, in a court proceeding, would not be able to rely on the defense of sovereign immunity, particularly given the intentional misrepresentations contained in the press release.

Mr. Mehdizadeh has claims for, among other things, defamation, tortious interference with prospective economic advantage, intentional infliction of emotional distress, and violation of Business and Professions Code Section 17200. Through counsel,

Mr. Mehdizadeh demands an immediate retraction of the press release.

If the DCA chooses not to retract the press release, then Mr. Mehdizadeh will seek damages for (1) emotional distress; (2) humiliation; (3) injury to reputation; and (4) economic losses. You should be aware that Mr. Mehdizadeh has incurred monetary losses based on denied business opportunities due to the press release. Mr. Mehdizadeh will pursue these remedies in an unlimited civil case with damages in excess of $25,000.

Please advise me by December 23, 2013, if you wish to resolve this matter prior to litigation.

Within days of the letter, the online link to the press release put out by the DCA was made inactive so people searching for the release could no longer find it within online archives for the county of Los Angeles. I was also informed that Joe had retired. These two events caused me to cease pursuing any civil remedy against the county of Los Angeles for what had transpired, and I focused my attention back to running Medbox full time, without distractions.

The criminal case against me was over, and I was worth hundreds of millions of dollars as the founder of a successful, publicly traded company that was the toast of Wall Street and our happy shareholders. In my mind, I had ventured through hell and come out on the other side victorious. However, as I would find out later, the damage that Joe and the DCA had intended had already been done. Their comments, along with Medbox's miraculous share price, made me an easy target for extortionists and short-bloggers alike, looking to hurt and discredit me and the company for their own financial gain. At that point, I was thirty-five years old and had amassed four felony convictions. On paper, I looked like a career criminal. However, to those who knew me, I was extremely good-natured, honest, and an impeccable businessman.

CHAPTER 8

───── ✣ ─────

How I Hit My Stride in Business and Found My Purpose

<u>The universe takes care of givers, not takers.</u>

IN THE MIDDLE of 2009, before I had been charged with the fifteen-count criminal indictment, I'd received a denial of a patent on the cannabis-dispensing, biometric machine I had invented. My patent attorney told me I should consider abandoning the idea because an appeal was not viable. About an hour later, I threw the patent application into the trash. And that's where it sat, staring at me, until I felt compelled to pull it out.

I could feel my mother from beyond the grave, urging me, "Pick it back up!" So I called my patent attorney and said I knew it was a long shot but thought the appeal was worth filing. More than a year later, my patent was approved! When that happened, I saw clear sailing ahead. I thought I had found my calling.

Up until this point, my company had been called Prescription Vending Machines, a name that shared my own initials: PVM. But now, I wanted to get away from the association with vending machines. That's how the company became Medbox. By the time my patent was granted, I'd gotten plenty of notoriety and media traction, but I had never actually sold any machines. In early 2008, when I just had one prototype in operation, other dispensary operators were calling us, trying to buy machines. But I hadn't yet begun mass-producing them, and I wasn't too keen on having machines out for public consumption yet. We didn't yet have a more open-minded DEA overlooking the cannabis industry.

By early 2010, the industry was booming. The political backlash had abated with the election of Obama, who was more lenient on the industry, and so, in turn, was the DEA. The time was right to start thinking about manufacturing and marketing the machine. But before I looked for a manufacturer, I got in touch with the DEA, which had confiscated my first machine. It's important to meet your opponents head on. I wanted an opportunity to explain my project, let the DEA know what I'd learned from what I'd been through, and give it a sense of why I was doing what I was doing. I hadn't been given a chance to say anything previously. At that time, there had been no room for discussion on the matter.

I sent an e-mail to the head investigator at the DEA, who had been in touch with me years prior, saying, in effect, "Here is my project; these are the benefits of my machine, and here's how we mitigate the risks. This machine helps dispensary operators demonstrate compliance more efficiently. My heart is in the right place, and I'm in it for the right reasons."

The DEA investigator e-mailed me back: "Glad to see you're doing well. Oh, and by the way, we still have some computers of yours that were confiscated during the investigation, and they're available to be picked up." He didn't address anything I had said in my e-mail, and I didn't expect him to. As far as I was concerned, it wasn't necessary. I saw his e-mail as a positive gesture. The government sentiment toward medical cannabis had begun to shift.

Now it was time to look for a manufacturer. I had originally used one in Illinois, but this time, I wanted someone local so I could make sure it accurately reproduced the vision I had for the machine. I also wanted something more modern in function and appearance and with more bells and whistles. Online, I found AVT Inc., in Corona, California. Its CEO, Shannon, and I hit it off right away. I also met one of the main sales reps. AVT became an exclusive manufacturer for my company only and built a prototype.

Securing a manufacturer was a great load off my mind. There was still some stigma surrounding the medical-cannabis industry, and I'd been uncertain about whether I could find a willing partner. Absolutely elated,

I finally felt like my vision would come to fruition. AVT had no idea what the agreement meant to me, and I didn't let on. In a situation like that, you don't want to let vendors know that you need them more than they need you.

I'd approached AVT in the most professional manner possible and made sure the company understood that the machine was actually a security-and-control protocol rather than a pot-vending machine. The medical-cannabis industry is often the butt of jokes. Part of our daily process at Medbox was educating people about what we did and showing them how it wasn't that different from the measures hospitals have in place for controlling sensitive medications.

Typically, a manufacturer requires mass production, which can be very costly. I didn't have that problem, because AVT's infrastructure allowed companies like mine on a bootstrap budget to start out extremely small and scale up. Without AVT, Medbox wouldn't have been the success it ultimately became.

The first piece of the puzzle was in place—a good partner. This set my direction. Had I been unable to find a manufacturer, I would have had a nonstarter on my hands—the equivalent of an exotic automobile without an ignition key. For the drive back to Los Angeles after my meeting with AVT, I jumped into my Porsche 911 Carrera, turned the music up, and started cruising. I love nice cars, and on that day in particular, the ride was especially sweet. It was one of those moments when everything in the universe aligned, and I felt like I was exactly where I should be in my life.

AVT's willingness to make the machines as I needed them was only half the battle, though. The other half was to create a market for my product. My invention had received a lot of media attention in 2008, and I knew dispensaries would want the machine. But first, I had to refresh everyone's memory about the technology. I didn't hire a professional marketing firm. Instead, I logged onto Vistaprint.com and created my own postcards with a picture of the machine from back in 2008. Then I assembled a list of US dispensaries and did a mass mailing.

My decision to do an old-school mass mailing rather than use a more sophisticated form of marketing arose from my desire to let the industry know that these machines were back on the market and I was running with them. I didn't see the point in expensive pay-per-click advertising when I could market my invention directly to my target demographic. My campaign was successful. From the thousands of mailers I sent out, I got thirty or forty leads. That's a pretty good response rate for a mass mailing. When people received the mailers, their curiosity was piqued. They would call me and say, "I remember this machine from CNN years ago. How much does it sell for?"

I started a grassroots campaign and became very well known among local dispensaries. In this way, I began establishing the brand. Once the very first machine was built, I sold it to a Los Angeles dispensary operator—my first client. I had helped to get this dispensary established in 2009 while in my role as licensing consultant. They appreciated my technology and wanted to be the first dispensary in Los Angeles to showcase the machine.

In April of 2010, I was featured on CNBC. The way the interview came about was actually through a fluke. The reporter had been writing an article on the state of the medical-cannabis industry in Los Angeles and had happened to stumble upon the dispensary that had my new machine. The reporter had asked what it was, and the manager explained that it was the very first machine of its kind. The reporter then contacted me. The media story about a cannabis vending machine yielded a very cool two-and-a-half-minute clip of me talking about what I was trying to do with my invention.

The reporter asked how I thought the DEA viewed it, and I answered, "I believe they would be fine with it because, at the end of the day, my heart is in the right place on this project. This machine doesn't make it easier to access cannabis. In fact, if anything, it's just the opposite!"

At that point, the machine was still self-service. It was located in a restricted-access area of the dispensary, but patients accessed the machine the same way as they had the original: with fingerprints and a swipe card.

That's how it all started in 2010. After selling about two dozen machines in Los Angeles and the surrounding areas, I realized that the self-service aspect of the machine wasn't particularly customer friendly. It seemed cold to have the patients interacting with the technology on their own.

At that point, my thinking shifted: let's keep the human interaction in the equation. The patients wouldn't have to directly interface with the machine; it could be behind the counter with an attendant to make sure the patients got what they wanted. This new method would be a more customer-friendly approach while retaining all the security and transparency the technology brought to the table. There was also a secondary issue on my mind: state legislators could negatively view a system where patients had direct access to the machines. I figured that out in 2010, when a company spokesperson did some media interviews in Arizona, after it passed medical-cannabis legislation. A machine behind the counter would therefore offer a double benefit—it would be more customer friendly and less antagonistic to legislators. It wouldn't look like a street-corner vending machine. The media was already drawing that comparison, and I didn't want to give them any more ammunition.

We were a consulting and technology company. Any tech company has to make sure the technology is relevant and useful and is not a social leper. With the new model in place, we covered both of those bases equally well.

In late 2010, I had the idea to blend what I had been doing in 2009 with what I was now doing. In 2009, I'd helped new dispensaries with my consulting business, and now I was marketing my machines to existing operators. But the price tag didn't make sense for them. When I didn't get traction with existing dispensaries, I decided to flip my whole business plan to gear it toward entrepreneurs just entering the business. From that line of thinking, the model evolved into what it later became, and under that model, the company flourished.

I wanted to attract a certain kind of entrepreneur—those who cared about paying taxes and wanted to run their dispensaries in complete compliance. I started putting "business opportunity" ads on various websites. I was already known in Los Angeles, so people gravitated toward me to help them build new dispensaries.

I offered a package deal for my technology plus licensing and building the dispensary—a turnkey model with my technology built in. Instead of trying to convince existing dispensaries that they needed my technology, I made my job easier by bringing in new people not already familiar with the business and used to bad operating habits.

Medbox's clients were traditional professionals—doctors, lawyers, pharmacists, and so on. I liked the idea of working with professionals because I knew they wouldn't negatively impact my business with their actions. They had as much to lose as I did if they didn't stay above board—namely, their main careers.

With the turnkey model geared toward professionals, my tech company was able to make money in its first year of operation in an extremely volatile industry. At the height of what many would call a recession, we had revenues of $1.1 million for 2010. We also had a good year in 2011 through licensing dispensaries in Arizona. That's where I met Dr. Bruce Bedrick, who later became the CEO of Medbox.

Bruce was a resident of Arizona. He had started out as a client when he sold his chiropractic business in 2010 and wanted to get into another business. He heard about Medbox and called upon us to help him start up in California. He and I hit it off very well. Before Arizona even passed its medical-cannabis laws in November 2010, we were already discussing a working relationship and how we could help people in Arizona get licensing and establish their clinics if the law were to pass.

Arizona passed its legislation during those thirteen days I was awaiting bail, so I had to hear about it in jail. Bruce was already a client and was becoming a friend, but he couldn't reach me. He was told simply that I had had a family emergency. Interestingly, the Arizona law allowing medical-cannabis dispensaries had failed—until one day later, when a recount of the state ballots reversed everything. Apparently, the law had succeeded by a very slim margin of less than five thousand votes.

If not for the passage of the Arizona law, Medbox would have failed. My pending criminal case had caused me to limit my business activities in the state of California, which was the revenue channel and market Medbox had tapped up to that point. The Arizona legislation created a new market for Medbox. During 2011, we signed a lot of Arizona clients and were thriving—until June, when there was a challenge by the governor of Arizona. The licensing period for medical-cannabis dispensaries was put on hold while she tried to overturn the new law.

For the next year, we kept our clients informed through conference calls every few weeks. All the while, I had a good feeling that the program would be reinstated. My thinking was, you can't stop progress. A democratic vote in a democratic system should be adhered to.

After all the time, energy, and money we'd spent preparing our clients' applications with the state and all the money our clients had invested, it seemed inconceivable to me that the law would not be upheld. There would have been an outcry from the citizens of Arizona. Sure enough, a judge saw it that way too, and a year after it was put on hold, the law was reinstated.

I'd hired a paralegal, and together, we spent a year and a half preparing the applications for our clients. So, by the time the law was reinstated in 2012, we were ready to go. Of the 490 applications filed, approximately 80 were from clients of Medbox.

Arizona was the first state to license dispensaries. Knowing there would be a lot of competition for the licenses, they created a lottery system. All applications that met the necessary criteria—which all of ours did—were entered into a ping-pong-ball lottery that was streamed live over the Internet. Our strategy was to file multiple applications per client to give them the best shot. For example, if a prospective dispensary had five partners, I filed separate applications for each instead of putting all five on the same application. The rules stated that the same person could not apply twice in the same zone within the state, but there was no prohibition against splitting partners up on to separate applications. It wasn't about breaking the rules—it was about figuring out how to stay within the rules while seeking out the competitive advantage.

We did really well for our clients. They received twenty of the ninety-seven Arizona licenses. We built out their dispensaries—we took care of construction, alarms, and secure-access doors; we supplied the furniture; and, of course, we provided them with our state-of-the-art Medbox dispensing machines. Since 2011, Medbox generated millions of dollars in revenue from Arizona alone and made its clients there millionaires in the process. Dispensaries there currently market for anywhere between $2 million and $10 million for well-established dispensaries in the coveted Phoenix metro area.

My direct service to the many Medbox clients in Arizona and seeing their matters through, while also being the subject of a fifteen-count criminal indictment in California, is an accomplishment that I am extremely proud of to this day. At that point, in 2013, Medbox was by many accounts the most successful consulting firm in the burgeoning medical-cannabis industry.

CHAPTER 9

— ✂ —

Taking Medbox Public Creates
Investor Euphoria

Some say that entrepreneurs jump off a cliff and build a plane on the way down. To survive the fall, visualize the life you want, stay focused, persevere through challenges, and achieve the best version of the life you can.

AT THE END of 2011, I took a meeting with Shannon Illingworth at AVT headquarters in Corona, California. Shannon had founded the publicly traded AVT; I felt that this status gave the company a certain mystique. Shannon wanted to introduce me to Mindful Eye, a separate public company under his control. Its business model involved consumers downloading movies onto USB drives through kiosks at busy public places, like grocery stores, airports, and malls, for later viewing. I wasn't passionate about this model, but I saw the business as a blank canvas ready to be molded into something that I could put my energy behind. The idea for my private company to become public germinated in my head. It became clear to me that Mindful Eye could one day be known as Medbox.

To take a private company public, there are many things to investigate and consider. It typically requires anywhere from $0.5 million to $1 million in legal and other administrative fees, and it's a very long and time-intensive process. Considering the time and the cost involved, going public through traditional channels may not be worthwhile for a smaller company. But a reverse merger is a way for a private company to have a public-company presence for a fraction of the resources required for traditional initial public offerings (IPOs).

The recipe is fairly straightforward. A private company proprietor negotiates for an acquisition by an existing public company. The private company's management team may assume management and control of the new company. The reverse merger, however, is somewhat stigmatized as a corner-cutting way to go public, a perception intensified when companies executing reverses then seem to pump and dump. In this fraudulent practice, companies encourage investors to buy shares in them to inflate the price artificially, and then insiders sell their own shares while the price is high. Unfortunately, this does happen.

The stigma of reverse merger wasn't a problem for me, though, since, as a student of the cannabis industry, I was savvy enough to know that a traditional IPO was not an option because the federal government considered these businesses illegal enterprises. The fact that Medbox was not in the business of selling, cultivating, or marketing cannabis didn't change my thinking on the topic. Companies simply providing ancillary support services for the industry were commonly classified federally under the same label. I had to do a reverse merger to go public then. Although, within the last two years, the SEC has approved registration statements for public companies that actually engage in the sale and production of cannabis. The industry is indeed moving at light speed—although I have yet to see a cannabis company succeed at an IPO.

If a public company hasn't really found its purpose and is in need of direction, the reverse-merger scenario can truly be a win-win for all parties, including the public company's existing shareholder base. The existing shareholders want to see a return on their current investment in the dormant public company. If the private company it merges with is generating revenue, it benefits them, and my company was already profitable. It's hard enough to accomplish that, and many entrepreneurs are content with it. But I had a bigger vision in mind.

Plenty of entrepreneurs buy majority stakes in publicly traded companies, take over management, and use them as investment vehicles, heavily marketing their stock. This was especially true in the cannabis sector at the time that Medbox went public, but it still is today. But these entrepreneurs apply untested business models in public companies and unleash them on the investment community, creating false and unproven investment vehicles. One reason why penny stocks (which are widely defined as stocks worth less than five dollars per share) have such a bad reputation is that some of the entrepreneurs are all hype and no substance.

My idea had been to build a solid private company first. Admittedly, I had not originally aspired to go public, but when I saw what Shannon had done with AVT, I looked at him as a mentor and thought I could learn a lot from him. When he offered me half ownership of Mindful Eye, for $25,000, I jumped all over it. Within a month, I had convinced him to abandon the movie-download kiosk idea, to rename the company Medbox, and change the ticker symbol to MDBX.

Shannon was an easy sell on rebranding the company and changing its focus. He had witnessed firsthand how I had gotten my private company off the ground and flourishing. I had conducted countless media interviews and was a very good spokesperson for my company. I had also informed Shannon of the burgeoning cannabis industry and that it was poised for growth like the alcohol industry after Prohibition. However, I guarded my private company carefully. I wasn't completely sold on merging the operating histories of the two companies. Sure, the company shared names now, but my thought was to develop Medbox as a separate public company that would do exclusive business with my own company.

A few months after the rebranding, however, I finally was ready to take the plunge. Shannon was initially skeptical of the merger idea. Eventually, I transferred interest of the private company for a $1 million note (to be paid a year later in cash if the public company had it) and two million shares of public-company stock. We had Shannon's attorney, Phillip, handle the merger.

I felt an overwhelming sense of accomplishment. I had taken my life of lemons and made myself a tall glass of lemonade. I had invented a product, patented it, produced it, took it to market, and built a booming business around my invention that was relevant and viable. Taking the company public was prestigious, and it gave me more incentive to climb higher. Being public meant we could raise more money from investors and expand into additional market segments, which suited us just fine. The company had operated on a bootstrap budget since I had founded it in 2010, which meant we were often stretched thin despite our profitability.

There was one problem, though: market awareness of the company's stock! Mindful Eye's shares had rarely traded in the public markets. Market awareness and support are crucial components to public-market success, and the way a company presents itself to prospective investors is also critical. I didn't see our situation as a huge problem, though, and focused my full attention on developing the business with the philosophy "if you build it, they will come." That attitude served me well. I focused on performing for clients and communicating the company's results in press releases so that investors looking for a new and dynamic company could easily find us.

During 2012, I had spent months grooming the company for greatness. We were truly doing great things for our clients and the cannabis industry as a whole. By August, I decided to approach Shannon about buying him out of Medbox. I had begun to feel that he had some fast-and-loose business practices. While none of them included criminal conduct, I realized that with my own criminal matter pending, I had no margin for error in my business associations. I wanted an amicable settlement. Shannon seemed like a nice guy, and after all, AVT still manufactured Medbox's machines, so I had to tread lightly.

I offered Shannon $50,000 in cash and a $450,000 future note plus 250,000 shares of Medbox stock. He was initially unenthusiastic, but I was persistent. Shannon had known about my pending criminal matter, and I explained that this meant I had to go it alone. I also pointed out that my situation could eventually have negative repercussions on his own business reputation. The deal was great for him, since it would return many times his original investment in Mindful Eye and also give him a small equity stake in Medbox; he could benefit if the company and stock performed under my guidance.

By late August 2012, I was the majority owner and controller of Medbox. The market for its stock was stagnant, and it traded lightly and sporadically every few days or sometimes weeks. I believed that the company was doing all the right things; we didn't engage some slick investor-relations firm and promise the moon and the stars to our shareholders. We didn't do anything illicit to get the company on investors' radars. Those types of marketing campaigns reeked of impropriety, and I kept in mind my lack of margin for error. I chose very carefully how the company disseminated corporate communications as well as its business associations.

I wasn't all that surprised that our stock wasn't more active, since I hadn't actively promoted it. The fact was that I hadn't found an investor-relations firm that didn't give me the creeps. It was hard to find one that actually had a network of sophisticated, liquid-investor contacts who were happy to receive information on new opportunities. Those are few and far between in penny-stock land.

However, the company had a fantastic website and corporate presence. It was the only company in the sector that had a patented product and was generating millions of dollars in revenue, performed well for clients, and had turned a profit in each of its first two years. I wanted anyone visiting the website to know that we were the best and brightest public company in the cannabis sector. It prominently displayed our patented technology and our stock data and graph; it discussed our consulting services for aspiring canna-business entrepreneurs, and it had a page dedicated to the many media appearances and press releases showcasing the company's progress and forward momentum. I was intimately involved in every corporate decision, marketing effort, website-design element, business-development nuance, media interview, and corporate communication at Medbox. I communicated that we were the real deal and were on the ground floor of something big—the next great American industry during its formative years.

Sometimes, perception dominates reality. If you are a savvy business-person, you can use that to your benefit. But, corporate positioning and perceived dominance of the industry aside, my running joke at headquarters was that we were the best public company that no one in the investment community knew about. Then I caught a break. My careful work yielded a referral by a colleague to a reporter from MarketWatch, a subsidiary of the *Wall Street Journal*, who was writing an article about public companies jockeying for a position in the legal-cannabis business sector. I quickly e-mailed the reporter, introduced myself and Medbox, and told him I would make myself available to give him insight into the industry and the company. He was interested.

The stage had been set. While I had no idea what the exact angle of the article would be, I knew that a mere mention of Medbox in a mainstream online venue like MarketWatch would be enormous exposure for us, introducing the company to a slew of day traders and long-term investors alike, looking to pour money into the next big thing—the Green Rush! I had built Medbox on the prediction that the forward momentum in the legal-cannabis sector would lead to mainstream acceptance. There was increasing social tolerance of the plant and market acceptance of the industry.

Mr. Quentin Fottrell interviewed me. When I asked about what exactly the article would cover, his response was vague. He said it named a few public companies in the cannabis industry and detailed some of their products and services. My next question might have been what made a difference in Medbox's future. I asked if its ticker symbol, MDBX, would be featured. He paused for a moment and replied that he hadn't thought to add any tickers to the article but that he would take it up with his editors.

A few days later, the article was live on the home page of MarketWatch: "How to invest in legalized marijuana." I was absolutely elated to see that Medbox had been prominently featured among a few other companies in the sector. Its ticker symbol, linking the article to the company's financial reporting pages, had also been featured! Anyone reading the article could also hover over the ticker link and receive nearly real-time information on Medbox's stock performance that day.

I was even quoted in the piece! The paragraph discussing Medbox read as follows:

> *For regular investors looking to get in on the action—and without having to actually grow or sell drugs—there are several small-cap stocks that stand to gain from cannabis's growing acceptance. Medbox [MDBX], an OTC stock with a $45 million market cap, for example, sells its patented dispensing machines to licensed medical-cannabis dispensaries. The machines, which dispense set doses of the drug, after verifying patients' identities via fingerprint, could potentially be used in ordinary drugstores too, says Medbox founder Vincent Mehdizadeh. Based in Hollywood, Calif., the company already has 130 machines in the field, and it expects to install an additional 40 in the next quarter. "The smart money is trying to help with compliance and transparency," Mehdizadeh says.*

Being mentioned on MarketWatch was one thing, but actually having Medbox featured along with a quote from me was quite another. Even after processing the fact that the article would have an immediate impact on my company, I still had no clue of what was yet to come.

Almost immediately after the article went live, Medbox's stock began to find its market, increasing its price enormously. Within hours, it had gone from a few dollars to over ten dollars per share! If that wasn't enough, the next day, the stock climbed to $215 per share at one point, making the company worth billions of dollars based on market capitalization (and me an overnight billionaire as the majority shareholder with more than forty million shares)!

While I was elated at the unprecedented attention Medbox's stock was receiving, I immediately started strategizing on the company's corporate message to the public and its shareholders, following such dramatic popularity. I was concerned about the potential for seasoned day traders to benefit from such wild price swings and the average investor in the public markets getting caught up in the "Green Rush" euphoria after a number of recent articles and media reports about states like Colorado and Washington voting to legalize recreational cannabis.

I saw the attention as a blessing and a curse because having to justify our share price could bring disfavor. It was difficult to figure out an appropriate course of action since a company's valuation is sometimes based on positioning, brand identity, and what the market perceives the company might be worth in the future. A company's board of directors and management publicly panning its own share price is something that no one in our advisory core had ever seen before. This made the decision even more nerve-wracking. I decided to release a company announcement responding to the unprecedented rise in Medbox's share price on the newswire the following day. In part, it read as follows:

"While we are pleased by the share attention, Medbox shares have traded between $2.75 and $3.45 over the past several months. Our fundamentals and market potential are improving, especially with the potential of our new Rx product line, but we temper investor expectations at present price points."

In the days since the article, Medbox has seen their stock rise, giving the company a market cap of $2.26 billion. The management of Medbox is concerned about the sudden and pronounced increase in their stock price and is taking steps to reduce these tremendous price swings.

"We will take steps to attempt to avoid a roller-coaster syndrome, with the stock rising and falling in dramatic fashion," Medbox company founder, Vincent Mehdizadeh stated.

Additionally, the company is investigating means to minimize any potential shareholder losses should the stock price fall rapidly.

"We are in discussions with our attorneys to determine if we can reward our early investors who believe in our company, by giving them company-owned shares should the price they bought at fall significantly," Mehdizadeh said. *"That's what classy companies do."*

As expected, the release received mixed reviews from the public, with some questioning why a company's management would choose to deflate its own stock price. A few critics marveled, while others complimented the company's management for honesty and integrity. I had always aimed to build a brand with longevity and relevance, and to do that, you need to make sure that the corporate image stays clean and do right by the company's clients and shareholders. So, instead of popping champagne and toasting to my newfound megawealth, I instead sought to "temper investor expectations" and publicly announce that we were not yet a billion-dollar company but had promise in a newly emerging industry that was picking up steam.

In the hours following the release, the stock price declined to about twenty dollars per share but surprisingly bounced back and actually stayed above fifty dollars for the next few days. That's when Quentin, the journalist from MarketWatch, reached out to me for a follow-up article regarding Medbox's tremendous market activity. I felt blessed that I could keep the interaction going with such an esteemed and relevant source, who wrote for one of the biggest financial news outlets in the world. The interview focused on the company's decision to dampen investor euphoria. The next day, on November 19, 2012, Quentin published "Marijuana-dispenser stock gets too high." It read, in part, as follows:

A company that creates medical-cannabis dispensing machines says its stock is getting way too high.

Medbox MDBX, shares surged 3,000% this week—from roughly $4 Monday to $215 Thursday—before falling to $100 after executives sought to dampen investor enthusiasm.

In a news release today, the company said that the stock's rocket launch, which sent its market cap skyrocketing from $45 million at the start of the week to a staggering $2.3 billion, was ignited by a MarketWatch story Tuesday on how to invest in legalized cannabis. (That's about double the market capitalization of retailer Jos. A. Bank Clothiers.) The stock, which fell around 50% in early trading Friday, still hovers at $100. "We believe an appropriate trading range is between $5 and $10 but, alas, the market will do what it will do," says Medbox founder Vincent Mehdizadeh.

The company says it's also investigating ways to minimize any potential shareholder losses. Medbox is in discussions with its attorneys to see if it can reward early investors with company-owned shares should the price they bought at in recent days fall significantly. "We don't want those investors to have sour feelings about what happened," Mehdizadeh says. "Obviously day traders are having a field day lately trading our stock."

But it's very risky to invest in drugs prohibited at a federal level, experts say. Nearly 500 of the estimated 3,000 dispensaries nationwide have closed or were shut down by the federal government in the past year, according to StickyGuide.com, an online directory for medical cannabis dispensaries. Currently, Medbox has 130 dispensers in the field and is due to install 40 more next month, and says it's looking at the broader pharmaceutical market.

The overwhelming sentiment was that Medbox was a speculative investment and that buying its shares on the open market at anything over "five and ten" dollars was risky for investors. However, the warnings to proceed with caution fell on deaf ears, and the company's stock price kept gaining momentum. Media appearances on CNBC's *Closing Bell with Maria Bartiromo* followed, along with others on the Fox News Channel, Bloomberg Television, and a swarm of outlets clamoring to learn more about Medbox and talk about the legal-cannabis industry. Fox News Los Angeles even came to Medbox headquarters to talk about the company's technology, the legal-cannabis industry, and of course our "miraculous Wall Street story," as the reporter called it.

The industry itself was front-page news because of recent medical-cannabis approval votes in Massachusetts and recreational initiatives approved in Colorado and Washington. The momentum was awe-inspiring, and the go-to choice for media interviews was Medbox. By the end of 2012, Medbox's shares were trending upward, and we finished the year near a hundred dollars per share! I was worth about $2 billion, and the company was worth almost $3 billion! I was absolutely elated at the market reaction to a company I had founded with blood, sweat, and tears. I had experienced success that only a few entrepreneurs ever do.

The feeling around Medbox headquarters in West Hollywood, California, was positively electric! I had assembled a trustworthy, good-natured team that deserved to taste success every bit as much as I did. Prior to Medbox's stock finding its groove, I had given, from my own holdings, between five thousand and ten thousand shares to each of the company's consultants, sales associates, and employees. I also gave Dr. Bruce Bedrick, our CEO, five hundred thousand shares. He had been instrumental in the company's successes in Arizona.

Last, I gave my father fifty thousand shares, telling him that one day they could be worth something, and I hoped he could retire on my gift. Well, as fortune had it, the day came sooner than we had ever expected. The gift was worth a staggering $5 million at the end of 2012. My gifts to the company's staff and consultants had also surged in value. All the gifts had amounted to tens of millions of dollars, and I felt humbled that I had potentially changed these people's lives so dramatically. While only some at the office knew of my still-unresolved criminal matter, all believed in my abilities and knew how hard I had worked to make the company a success against all odds.

At the end of 2012, I told everyone I had given shares to, including my father, that they couldn't sell them for an entire year since they had come from an affiliate of the public company. They all agreed. I didn't want my gifts to negatively impact the company's market, even if I had given them months before there was even a semblance of a market for the stock.

As for Medbox, after the stock's notoriety, we were inundated with investor calls for direct purchase of shares. As a result, Medbox took in over $2 million in equity sales to accredited investors in November and December 2012. These investors bought restricted, long-term shares at a significant discount: they had to hold them for at least one year per SEC regulations. With this infusion of capital, Medbox was flush with cash and a force to be reckoned with in its industry. Other companies began to take notice and wanted to work with us. Many aspiring entrepreneurs peddled some "revolutionary" idea for sale; other companies wanted to be acquired and get bailed out of their issues. It was time-consuming and sometimes frustrating, but we answered all calls cordially. Especially at the time, the legal-cannabis industry was small, so it was important to us not to be seen as high and mighty. The jealousy factor was starting to create waves, and I certainly didn't want to add fuel to it.

As for my newfound extraordinary wealth, it left me relatively unchanged. Of course, I was happy about the possibilities it would bring to my life, but I stayed centered and realized that Medbox had a lot to live up to. Its enormous stock price would need to be backed up with solid performance for the shareholders and company to benefit on a long-term basis. My fifteen-felony-count criminal case still loomed and was on my mind constantly, although in my heart, I always knew that I had a solid defense and that the case would eventually be resolved successfully.

At the time, I was renting a two-bedroom apartment overlooking the ocean in Malibu and drove the Porsche Panamera that I had had since 2011. When I could have started selling my own shares in the public markets, I didn't. Millions of dollars were there for the taking, but I opted not to be an entrepreneur who cashed in at the first available opportunity. I chose to remain in integrity and refused to give in to temptation. I decided to wait another year—until I was 100 percent certain that the swarms of investors in discounted long-term Medbox shares had the opportunity to make a profit.

It was a tough decision, but I knew it was the right one. I also wanted to avoid any suspicions of a pump and dump. While I publicly cautioned investors about the risks of Medbox stock in the public markets, I wanted to remove the potential of any future doubt for a regulator who might question why I sold my own stock. I felt that this way, my motivations and ethics as a founder and majority shareholder would be clear.

I rewarded myself by taking $100,000 of the $1 million that Medbox owed me on the promissory note from selling my private company to it. Though the company could have paid the whole note, I didn't want to take operating capital away from Medbox. With the money, I bought myself a brand-new 2013 Porsche 911 Carrera. The car was absolutely gorgeous, and I loved every minute behind its wheel. It was my birthday gift to myself. I had turned thirty-four on Christmas Day 2012, and as far as I was concerned, I deserved it!

In December 2012, I transferred an additional seven million shares to Bruce for his continued services to the company from my personal holdings to avoid diluting the public shares. Bruce was doing most of Medbox's media appearances, was pivotal in day-to-day decisions as the company's CEO, and was one of the directors of the board. Bruce was charismatic, smart, and an excellent spokesperson for the company. I believed that he needed a large stake in Medbox for the company to continue to succeed. Though this amounted to a substantial reduction of my shares, I was content being worth about $2 billion and having a happy CEO help lead Medbox into the next growth phase. To me, it was always about being part of something real, relevant, and viable.

Of particular importance was that Shannon's former controlling shares of Medbox had included three million preferred shares that could be converted into fifteen million additional shares of common stock, along with three other certificates totaling an additional six hundred thousand common shares. There had also been a fourth share certificate that had been issued to a marketing company for services in the amount of 226,000 shares. Shannon and Phillip had told me that these shares could be transferred to another marketing company or other service provider of my choosing. At the time, August 2012, I felt this wasn't a huge concern.

When I became the single largest shareholder of Medbox, I held more than 30 million shares, not counting the 3 million preferred and the 826,000 shares available through those four other certificates. At that point, all the shares were worth very little, since the market for the company's stock was almost nonexistent. The three million preferred shares had thus far stayed in my filing cabinet at the office, and the rest of the certificates had stayed with Phillip for months, even after I bought Shannon out. However, by November 2012, the shares in Phillip's possession were worth a whopping $74 million!

I had asked Phillip for legal advice regarding all the certificate shares before I was ever involved with what was then Mindful Eye. Phillip had confirmed that the shares had been validly issued. Once I controlled the new company, he had verified that they were available to me to do with as I pleased. I asked if I could legally direct the shares held by the marketing company to a company owned by my then-girlfriend. He said, "Absolutely." She had witnessed my amazing rise to wealth and all the issues I had had to deal with in making Medbox a success while overcoming a mountain of personal obstacles.

My girlfriend's family was made up of humble, working-class people, and like most families, they struggled to make ends meet. She was a licensed real-estate agent at the time, and I knew that my gesture would change her family's lives forever. She was a good person who deserved a break. But rather than give her and her family shares out of my own holdings (which I could have lawfully done) for their emotional support of me over the years, I decided to direct the 226,000 marketing company shares to her company, under Phillip's supervision. She had always felt like she had underachieved as a businesswoman, and with this newfound wealth, she could jump-start her real-estate career by buying properties and managing the rental income, or whatever other ventures she felt worthwhile. I had always considered the good fortune I had in life to be the direct result of my positive influence on others' lives, so this was right up my alley and made me feel good. In early 2014, my girlfriend and I parted ways amicably. Her family was very appreciative for my support over the years and respected me tremendously.

I had also decided that for the benefit of the shareholders, I would retire (cancel) the six hundred thousand shares held in the other three certificates as well as the three million preferred shares. This meant that I caused the equivalent of 15.6 million additional shares, worth $1.5 billion that I could have added to my own holdings, to be deposited back to the company treasury. This reduced the number of issued and outstanding shares of the company's stock in that amount, benefiting all Medbox shareholders tremendously. When I advised Phillip I was retiring the shares, he asked why I would do such a thing. To him, it was throwing money down the drain, but in my mind, making that kind of grand gesture and announcing it in a press release would galvanize the company's market and demonstrate my generosity and respect for the company's shareholders. I was already worth billions. Having that high a percentage of the company's outstanding stock seemed greedy to me.

Before the end of the year, I had already begun strategizing what the company needed to do to keep its momentum going. We had gained all this attention and were no longer a penny stock, but Medbox was still a pink-sheet stock, which meant it was not subject to SEC-filing requirements. Medbox always voluntarily filed financials and disclosure statements publicly, giving it the classification of "OTC Pink—Current Information." However, I had always wanted more for the company and was determined to have it become an SEC filer. Even before the share price had skyrocketed, we had started the process of becoming a fully reporting company.

Phillip, who had remained as our corporate and SEC attorney, counseled that we had to have two years of the company's historical financials audited. The rest, he said, was simple paperwork. Phillip recommended an auditor, who began working with us in mid-2012. By the end of the year, the company had catapulted to fame and success, and I felt it was even more important to get the audit done and graduate from being a pink-sheet company with no reporting requirements and limited transparency to the investing public (a "stinky pinky," as some like to call it).

Although SEC filings are burdensome and costly, I had always envisioned its higher status for Medbox once I had learned the difference. Phillip had warned about the extra expenses and the scrutiny of every single move the company made, including that insider sales had to be disclosed to the public immediately. To me, it was a no-brainer if a company was engaged in the public markets, and especially in the legal-cannabis industry, to be subject to SEC reporting requirements. Either be a solid, transparent, and viable company that files with the SEC, or be one that would always be viewed as questionable by the investment community and public at large.

While we were having the company's audit completed, I hired an executive-recruitment service to find someone with public-company experience to help us navigate the minefields of protocol since neither Bruce nor I had such experience. I selected Will, a seasoned executive with over a decade of relevant experience; he joined us in January 2013. He had even founded a pet-insurance company that he took public. (He also claimed to be a PhD.) The pieces were all falling together so nicely. It seemed like a dream! At the same time, the nightmare that Joe, Abdul, and Abdul's attorney, Stanley, could pop up out of the woodwork at any time still loomed.

I worried that they could spread misinformation to the press, sending the Medbox share price plummeting and losing its shareholders a ton of money. I could see them trying to spite me under the guise of protecting the public from me, the alleged sociopath, after my much-publicized successes. This cloud over my head was hard to shake at times. I prayed to my mother every night and thanked the universe for blessing me with all my recent successes. I hoped that the hatred some people had in their hearts for successful people wouldn't rain on my parade and hurt others financially who were betting on Medbox's continued success.

CHAPTER 10

— ❀ —

Medbox Retains Its Multibillion-Dollar Market Valuation

Founding a successful company is 20 percent skill, 15 percent dedication, 10 percent luck, 5 percent pleasure, and 50 percent pain.

THE YEAR 2013 started just as well as 2012 had ended. Medbox was fielding media inquiries from local and national outlets looking to get the scoop on what many were calling _the_ stock story of 2012. I was still in shock but kept a very balanced approach to it all, understanding that the market for the company's stock was still unproven. And, just as easily as investors had propped the stock up to incredible levels, if sentiment for the company or the industry were to change, the price could just as easily diminish and deteriorate over time, or even overnight, depending on the circumstances. Despite repeated warnings to our public-market investors, they still bought Medbox stock at highs between twenty dollars and ninety-eight dollars during the first few months of 2013.

Living up to the hype became a seventy-hour-a-week job for me. The sheer volume of e-mails and phone calls from new and existing clients, prospective financiers to the company, investors who wanted direct stocks, and other hopefuls looking for working relationships or business synergies with Medbox was both remarkable and time-consuming. I needed assistance in managing it all and still had my criminal case pending. I hired Will to pitch in and help the company mature into a fully reporting SEC filer and no longer a pink-sheet company. Will jumped into the mix and showed tremendous promise, and Bruce and I were immediately happy with his direction and advice.

A couple of months in, I asked Will if he would replace me as a company director as I dealt with my pending legal issues. He gladly accepted, and I transferred him 2,500 Medbox shares from my personal holdings as a token of my appreciation. The shares were worth over $60,000 at the time, so it was by no stretch a small token. Will seemed stunned by my generosity, but in my view, it was an investment into Medbox's future.

Will struck me as a genuine guy with a pure heart but who had not hit his stride to become financially stable yet for whatever reason. He drove a beat-up, older automobile to work, but it could have been considered a classic of sorts, so it didn't make me think any less of him. I rationalized that maybe Medbox would be his home run, the vehicle with which he could finally attain financial independence. A talented executive just hitting his stride could be a real benefit to the company and its shareholders.

Will also interfaced with the company's auditor, Tim, to ensure that the audit and filing with the SEC were on track. I also wanted to improve the company's profile by retaining a firm that specialized in securities laws and regulatory requirements. Phillip was the solo practitioner we had inherited, but maturing companies tend to phase out weaker attorneys and consultants from their formative years (early on, they simply can't afford the big-name firms). Since Medbox had achieved a multibillion-dollar market capitalization, it needed to make this transition to show the investment community that it was progressing. We chose Ober Kaler, a Baltimore SEC firm.

The third item I felt was a must-have was an experienced chief financial officer to lead the company into the future. Tom came with over twenty years of business-management experience and had even worked as an auditor for KPMG (a Big Four firm) for ten years. (Put simply, the Big Four are the four largest international accounting firms.) In the first few months of 2013, I had tackled Medbox's three biggest issues. Business was booming, investor interest was constant, the market in the company's stock was stable, and my pending case showed signs of resolution on the horizon.

Yet, the threat of Joe, Abdul, and Stanley still lurked and the possibility of them publicizing my pending criminal matter. I had a couple of options for minimizing potential risk to the company and its shareholders; my being a majority shareholder could be an Achilles' heel for the company. The first option was to transfer the majority of my Medbox shares to a relative or a trustworthy friend. However, I didn't want to risk any suspicion of fraud. I then asked Bruce to take temporary possession of my majority holdings, but he brought up the point that the legal matter might not resolve in my favor. I said that in that case, the shares remained his. He accepted the proposal. After all, if I was sentenced to jail, he would have control of over a billion dollars' worth of shares. Meanwhile, I still had several million shares of Medbox stock in another holding company.

Within a few months of our Form 10 filing with the SEC, my case was resolved successfully, and I proudly stepped back as the majority shareholder in the company. We did have to report my new "convictions" to the SEC (and therefore the public) for transparency. Though my criminal record could still have resulted in negative media reports, it was still better than having the media report on a trial and speculate on whether the majority shareholder in a multibillion-dollar public company in the cannabis industry would go to jail! Without jail time, the news couldn't really hurt the company's market and sour shareholder sentiment. As long as we reported everything accurately to shareholders, I reasoned that the impact on share price wouldn't be dramatic. Shareholders seemed to understand the situation, and the market for the company's stock stayed constant and supportive.

In early 2013, Will was very helpful at Medbox, but he made some referrals to questionable consultants and legal advisors that had their own issues. One attorney had been sanctioned by the SEC, which Will disclosed to us. Bruce and I never really felt comfortable about using that attorney, so we didn't continue with him. Will also vouched for some prospective financing relationships and investor-relations services. However, after Bruce and I talked with them, we terminated our engagements with them within weeks. They had said things that just didn't make sense.

I wanted Medbox to be different from other public companies in the cannabis sector that spent more money on promoting their companies' stocks than actually running efficient and viable businesses, especially since we had garnered such organic popularity in our company's stock through media interviews. Regardless, we still appreciated Will because he seemed like he genuinely wanted to help the company succeed.

In April 2013, the company had a major scare that was partly Will's mistake. The auditor, Tim, whom Phillip had recommended, had completed his audit. Medbox issued a press release about it, naming Tim. The next day, a shareholder tipped us off that Tim was the subject of an SEC regulatory action for conducting an incorrect audit of another company. The shareholder had found this information on the Public Company Accounting Oversight Board (PCAOB) website. When we had hired Tim, this case against him had not yet been filed. I was shocked since I had asked Will to recheck the PCAOB website to make sure Tim's record was still unblemished.

After I told Will and Bruce the news, Will was profusely apologetic. He cowered in the corner of my office, looking dazed and bewildered. He said he had checked the site a week earlier and overlooked the charges against Tim. He stated that he had simply verified that Tim was still registered to conduct public-company audits and wasn't looking for any other disciplinary information. This was an absolute nightmare. The worst part was that Tim hadn't even let the company know of his pending issues. I immediately called him and followed with a very aggressive e-mail. Tim's response was, "I thought I had told you about it." It was one of the worst days of my career.

The company immediately issued a press release that it was seeking a new auditor, and we had a new firm in mind within days. However, our chief financial officer (CFO), Tom, had spoken with Tim and believed that he was innocent. Tim was still a licensed CPA and was able to conduct public-company audits while the case was pending. Tom made the case to Medbox management that we should continue with Tim under Tom's supervision. I was mortified by the entire situation but trusted Tom's instincts on the matter. In fact, I even rationalized that if Tim was under such intense regulatory scrutiny, his audits would be even more accurate.

Shortly thereafter, I began to notice irregularities in Will. He called me in tears one day and confided that his girlfriend might be dying of a rare skin disease and had to go in for additional tests. He said he had to leave the office and wouldn't be back that day. He had also spoken with Tom about it. I was sympathetic and told him he could take as long as he needed. From that point forward, something was strange about Will. He would come to the office, sit at his desk, and stare into space. He appeared visibly shaken in the following weeks. I chalked it up to him grieving in his own way and figured that he would get ahold of himself eventually.

On May 21, 2013, the periodic conference call with Bruce and Will went well; I had no indication that there were any morale issues. However, the following day, Will tendered his resignation and demanded $20,000 in severance. Bruce and I were absolutely stunned. In his resignation letter to Bruce, Will stated he could no longer work at Medbox and that I was the reason he was leaving. It was my first taste of corporate betrayal at Medbox, and it was quite bitter. To that point, nothing of the sort had ever occurred in my business career, so I took the news hard.

We rejected Will's severance demand, and things got testier. Will raised his demand to $80,000; otherwise, he would file complaints about me with the SEC, alleging that they would "harm the company" whether accurate or not. We again told him that we wouldn't pay him a dime. He hired a lawyer and then demanded $1.5 million. The attorney wrote me a personal e-mail to the effect of "We know you have money, Vince, and we know about your pending criminal matter. Pay this off and make it go away, or we'll sue the company and drag all your dirty laundry out for all to see."

They then filed a case against Medbox in Los Angeles Superior Court for damages upward of $1.5 million. The company pushed for arbitration, staying the court action. The company prevailed and received an award against Will for over $30,000 in legal fees, closing the matter. Will's parting shot was to file a whistleblower complaint against Medbox on the SEC website, sending a copy to the attorney who had helped us prevail in the arbitration.

The complaint stated that I had been selling Medbox shares secretly through my holding companies and that I was guilty of various securities violations. The complaint itself was incoherent. In the words of the company's attorney, it was "borderline nut bucket." I knew none of the various allegations had any truth, so while the company, its attorneys, and I took the matter seriously, there was nothing we could do at that point. Bruce and I both engaged independent SEC counsels to advise us on any potential exposure. In their inquiries, it appeared as if no government agency took Will's complaint seriously. Will then sent taunting e-mails to Bruce and me, saying that he was meeting with the FBI and SEC investigators. He told Tom, our CFO, that the FBI was going to raid us at any moment and that he should quit immediately. We shrugged and rolled our eyes in disbelief.

Meanwhile, it was business as usual at Medbox. We had clients to assist and piles of work to finish. After a while, Will's distractions became nothing more than white noise. In the weeks after Will's departure and after three long years of defending against criminal charges, I finally stepped back into a director seat at Medbox and was appointed chief operations officer (COO).

We discovered that Will had never held a PhD and that he had filed for bankruptcy just a few years before joining Medbox. The executive-recruitment service apparently had not known Will. More unsettling was that the SEC had delisted Will's former pet-insurance venture from the stock market for failing to file annual and quarterly reports. Additionally, in 2009, the Arkansas Securities Commission had filed an enforcement action against Will for selling unregistered promissory notes to retail investors. In 2010, the SEC had also barred Will's general counsel for two years from advising publicly traded clients, for drafting misleading filings for another client. That attorney was the one Will had tried to get Medbox to use.

In short, Will had failed to disclose any of his prior issues to Medbox, and as for the executive-recruitment service, it didn't do a good job vetting him at all. Entrepreneurs: learn from my mistakes and conduct professional background checks on all new prospective hires. Do not trust executive-recruitment firms to do the legwork for you. That simple step can be the difference between success and failure for your company.

CHAPTER 11

— ❧ —

The "Short" Reality of the Public Markets

In the game of craps, one type of person bets on success, and the other type of person bets on failure...the same is true in public markets.

WHEN SOMEONE ROLLS the dice at a craps table, he or she is on the "pass line," betting on the roll. The spectators around the table have a choice to bet on the roller's success or bet on the roller to fail. Those betting on the roller's failure bet on the "don't-pass line." Such people in our lives can be called "haters." In public-company life, they are called "shorters." Realizing that these forces exist and recognizing the positive and negative energy that these groups of people bring may help one to handle life's traumas and persevere through challenges more effectively. Knowledge is power, as they say. It makes becoming and staying successful in life and in business less of a crapshoot or gamble and more of a targeted outcome.

Shorters are investor-traders who target stocks that they believe are overvalued. They take a short position in the stock, borrowing the shares on margin from a brokerage firm. They rush out and sell the shares immediately, creating downward selling pressure on the stock and lowering its price. Shorters especially like to target stocks that have a weak, unproven, or untested market. These types of short sales sometimes cause legitimate investors, who are carefully watching a stock's performance, to sell off their positions in fear that the stock is on a downward spiral.

The shorters who just sold their broker-borrowed shares have to "return" them to the broker at some time in the future, so they wait for the stock price to go down even further. They then buy the replacement shares at the now-lower price to give back to the broker. Shorters make money on the difference between the sales price of the borrowed stock they sold and the price they end up actually buying the stock for once they decide to repay the borrowed shares. They count on the stock price going down. In their motivation to see the stock price go down, they may engage in online bashing of the company in chat rooms and on message boards.

Believe it or not, shorting is legal in most instances and is rampant in the public markets. Although rumormongering on Internet message boards or issuing false statements about a company or its principals to decrease a share price for financial gain is not legal, regulatory agencies usually have a tough time enforcing that without help—like the aggrieved company filing suit, identifying the usually anonymous online bashers, proving the inaccuracy of statements, proving that there is a shorting scheme, and proving damages related to the "short-and-distort" activities.

Needless to say, shedding light on an illegal shorting scheme is a very tedious process, and regulatory agencies are so busy policing other aspects of the public markets that illegal shorters remain unmonitored for the most part. I feel that regulatory authorities should focus more attention on it, since a company's market value can be unjustly destroyed by such illegal activities, causing huge losses for all the target company's shareholders.

During 2013, Medbox received a tremendous amount of media exposure at no charge, which I estimated at the time to be well worth over $10 million in market awareness. We had tremendous success in communicating our corporate message and extremely high visibility in a newly emerging industry that seemed to make the front-page daily. We were the voice of the industry, being featured in live television interviews seemingly every other week with sources such as Bloomberg, Fox Business, Huffington Post, CNBC, Fox News Channel, and many local-news channels in the Arizona and Southern California markets. The media's interest in our company's story, leveraged against the promise of the "next great American industry," made for a perfect storm, leading to consistently high share prices. I really started to believe in the company's market at that point. We had done the right things by warning investors about the speculative nature of the company's stock at its inflated levels. We had tried to build the best and most reputable company in the sector. Investors seemed to like our corporate story, that we generated revenue with a proven business model, and our impressive media exposure.

With the media exposure, high stock price, and an industry that was by all accounts "on fire," shorters began rearing their ugly heads. By the middle of 2013, a company shareholder alerted me to anonymous derogatory statements posted on Yahoo Finance and Investors Hub message boards dedicated to Medbox: "Medbox is a scam! They don't do anything," or "Look—Medbox doesn't have a product or service and they have no clients. They are lying to the world and are a scam!" Other posts stated that Medbox was "ripping off its shareholders." The same couple of posters were saying the same thing in a hundred different posts. The claims were patently false and obviously part of an organized shorting campaign.

I had built a solid company from scratch and was mortified at the possibility that the company's legitimate shareholders would see this nonsense and exit their stock positions. In addition, potential new shareholders seeing these baseless comments might avoid buying the stock out of fear that the claims might be true. Either could affect the share price. Decreased buying demand from new investors is exactly what the shorters were looking to accomplish.

I sprang into action, asking shareholders and clients to provide testimonials for Medbox and particularly about their experiences with Bruce and me. After compiling dozens of earnest comments, we issued a press release saying that we had added a testimonial section on our corporate website. Those testimonials, which I am proud to share, are below:

As an investor some four years ago by now, I have come to know Vincent very well over these many years thru thick and thin, and he has always come out on top when dealing with this old cranky hippy and has always tried to listen and understand where my issues have been and has always been professional with me as he has exceeded all of my expectations in growing the company to these levels in a relatively short time. He is forward thinking, and I believe he has his pulse on the industry and is a credit to the medical cannabis movement to help all patients get their medication in a safe environment. In other words he has his heart into what he knows will help countless folks have access to the herb/medication to help them live a better life.

C. Bateman, Redding, California
Client and Shareholder

I am a proud shareholder of Medbox stock. Since purchasing shares I have been extremely impressed with the professionalism in leadership of this company. They are pioneers in a field that will continue to grow as they set the example for the future of medical cannabis. I look forward to the journey ahead. Thank you for your perseverance and hard work that has made Medbox the leader in its field.

Pam King, Tucker, Georgia
Shareholder

We are extremely pleased with our investment in Medbox. Vincent has been extremely reachable at all times with any questions that we have had. He has always responded to all emails within the hour, I'm not sure how but that is one of the beauties of modern technology. We are so pleased with the progression

of Medbox and are looking forward to many successful years with the company!
D. Hope—Diamond Club Capital LLC, Florida
Shareholder

99.99999% approval rating from me. Your hard work & dedication shows it. Thanks for keeping me informed and answering any questions I may have.
C. Wilcox, Arizona
Client

What a ride! Ups and downs but always positive info for us shareholders. Always straight forward and no two people work harder than Dr. Bruce and Vincent keeping us informed and even answering emails themselves. They truly mean what they say. So appreciated on this end.
K. Steighner, Delaware
Shareholder

Dear Vincent Mehdizadeh,
As 2013 is drawing to a close, I am realizing that I need to say a few words to thank you for the opportunity you have provided me by being an investor in MDBX. When I initially spoke to you and decided to put my trust and faith in a young man with a bold idea, it was mid-2010 and I had no idea if you were going to be able to pursue the path you had planned, to make this business to a profitable enterprise. Nervously I agreed to invest a (for me) substantial amount of money.

Throughout that year and the following I happily discovered that you were good for your word, and that indeed due to your hard work and insight, the company actually made a profit from the start and continued to grow, even if the beginnings were tough and full of problems. You paid me dividends and kept me informed quarterly. When the transformation to MDBX occurred the business exploded. I would like to thank you for all that you have done to make this into the huge success that it has become today. You fought, rolled with the punches, and showed remarkable resilience and were able to change and adapt in a fast-paced developing business.

I thank you and applaud you for your hard work and ingenuity that you have shown for this company!

Sincerely,
P. Dellow, California
Shareholder

I have been part of a dispensary clinic project which I have received outstanding advice, clarification and ongoing support from Medbox throughout the project process. They are always looking out for their clients and continually strive to be at the forefront of this industry.
D Ritchie—Benson Management Services, LLC, Arizona
Client

Vincent and Bruce are proven professionals who are the leaders in this new technology and industry. I feel privileged to have been involved in such a blossoming endeavor. To have known

Bruce for most of my life is also very rewarding to follow his success.

Sincerely,

S. Harrison
Shareholder

We've had the pleasure of working, and continuing to work, with Vince and Dr. Bruce over the last several years. Companies, such as Medbox, that embrace forward-thinking patented technologies have significant competitive advantages in the marketplace. Vince and Dr. Bruce have developed innovative technologies that provide best solutions to measurably grow market share and mitigate risk through their attention to detail. Vince and Dr. Bruce continue to provide excellent customer service with a strong emphasis on access, convenience, process and best possible outcomes. Vince and Dr. Bruce are always willing to share their passion and non-stop work ethic to meet and exceed client expectations. We would rank the Medbox team as one of the most insightful and strategic teams with whom we've interacted.

Luke Kleyn—KMR Advisors
Shareholder

This letter of recommendation is for Medbox and Vincent Mehdizadeh as it relates to my business interactions with him. I find Vince to be honest and forthright in every aspect of our business relationship in the past four years. I am currently involved with Vince in another business venture and I would not hesitate to enter into future business ventures with him. Vince is hard working and has fantastic communication skills with all of his clients. Never once has Vince left me in the dark regarding any issues and

he always returned my inquiries in a timely manner. Please feel free to have potential clients contact me if they have any questions regarding Vince and his character.
Sincerely,
G. Stephen Johnson, California
Client

I am extremely grateful to Medbox for the most compliant medical cannabis dispensing machine and follow through with my investment group. The company has been growing strong and I am proud to be a company client and shareholder.
Dianne M., Arizona
Client and Shareholder

Vincent,
From all of us at BC Wellness Center, we would like to give you a special thank you for all the guidance and support you and your staff has given us in getting our dispensary up and operating with the technology you provide. You have gone above and beyond the call of duty to make sure we would be successful. We commend you on your efforts and dedication to Medbox and its clients.
Paul B.—BC Wellness Center, Black Canyon City, Arizona
Client

Vincent, Bruce and the team at Medbox continue to surpass my wildest expectations.

I spent many, many months evaluating Medbox as a potential investor in 2012. Thankfully I decided to give the folks at Medbox a shot prior to yearend. If I could turn back time I would have invested all my liquid resources in their business. Quite simply, Medbox has proven the single best investment for myself and my family. We are reaping the rewards of their intuition and ability to react properly as they break ground in an explosive market.

If you are looking for a real investment in an emerging market, look no further, the facts surrounding Medbox speak for themselves.
Matt Wood, Denver, Colorado
Shareholder

Vincent & Bruce, since day 1, have always put their client's interests ahead of their own. Thank you for making our project in Arizona a success under difficult circumstances.
J. Gigliotti, Arizona
Client

I have been involved with Vincent and Dr. Bruce since the investment group I am a part of was formed and hired their services in Arizona. They have always put their client's interests first and always produced on what was promised. Their advice has always been well reasoned and conservative. I value them as business consultants, entrepreneurs, and most importantly, as friends.
Dr. B. Cantor, Arizona
Client and Shareholder

Dr. Bruce and Vincent made it possible for me to be part of a groundbreaking industry of medical cannabis. I couldn't have done this without them and have learned a lot about the industry as a result. Looking forward to the future!

R. Phifer, Arizona
Client

I contacted what was then Vincent's private company, Medicine Dispensing Systems, back in 2011 so I could get started in the MMJ industry with a leader. Vincent has ushered me through every step of my desire to operate a new business and I credit him and Medbox with getting my small group of partners a dispensary license in Arizona. I couldn't have done it without him and his expert team. In fact, when the Arizona government challenged the dispensary program and licensing was halted for a year, Vincent gave me a personal loan of $7,000 in order to help me and my family out as we had invested most of our money into the new business and were not expecting the circumstances beyond everyone's control occurring at that moment. Vincent didn't have to do that but that's why Vincent is as successful as he is. He always tells me that in life people should pay it forward and not expect anything in return. Well, I can safely say that Vincent deserves all the success. He has worked hard for it!

L. Anderson—Benson Management Services, LLC, Arizona
Client

Medbox helped me secure a license in a very desirable location in metro Arizona. Unfortunately, my partner and I ran into some major impediments that almost cost us the opportunity to build our dispensary before the state imposed deadline. If we had not built our dispensary in time, we would have lost the license we worked so hard to secure. Vincent found out about the situation

and personally handled our build-out on credit until we were able to pay the company back. The company also filed a lawsuit for its clients and forced Arizona Department of Health Services to extend their deadlines an extra year. I owe my new business to Vincent, Dr. Bruce, and the gang at Medbox.
J. Chacon—Kind Meds, Arizona
Client

As a seasoned professional in real estate development, I have never seen so much red tape from local municipalities. Regardless of the excessive requirements, if it wasn't for Medbox stepping up and exceeding their contractual obligations, there is no way I would be able to obtain two dispensaries in Arizona. I am extremely fortunate and honored to say that I am part of the Medbox Family!
K. Voris, Arizona
Client

Tacky as it may sound, they had me from "Hello." When the good folks of AZ campaigned for MM, I was on board, and when it passed, I was both shocked & elated. I knew I wanted to be a part of it. But how? So, I reached out to Medbox. The staff was (and still is) professional, candid, and accessible. They treat people with respect & exhibit great patience, more than me, in dealing with doubters and haters. Many of my friends and colleagues were afraid to get involved in the industry. Medbox made me feel comfortable and confident about investing, and I did. They made no false promises nor guarantees of riches; they told it straight.

Well, several years later, my investment has paid off, and it may turn out to be life-changing for my family. The most important thing to me about Medbox is that the principals have remained open, candid, non-defensive and accessible. To this day, they respond to my phone calls or emails, which is truly amazing, given their success and their schedules. Medbox is their professional life, and they show unwavering dedication. In addition, their generosity is something I not only did not expect, but I've never seen anything like it before, i.e., they give back to the shareholders, and they give back to the community.

Both company heads, Vince & Dr. Bruce, have been great to me. They have worked tirelessly to grow the company and its value. Their actions show that they care about their customers and their shareholders. I give them and their company an unqualified endorsement!
Randy H., Arizona
Client and Shareholder

As one of the earliest and one of the largest Outside Investors of Medbox, I have a very strong statement to make. "Medbox is the best thing to ever come into my investment life." Every response has been quick and accurate to every question I've had. Sometimes the answer arrives before I have a chance to ask the question. Medbox has been totally transparent with facts and figures about the Company Operations. I am so glad that I invested in Medbox. The return has been phenomenal!

The Executives of Medbox have built a very solid foundation for future growth.
   This industry is in its infancy and Medbox is one of the solid leaders. (I believe the stock market agrees with me!)

Medbox has the tools and patents to grow the Company. They have the flexibility to make product changes as the market grows.

I wish I had bought more stock when I could.
J. Gavin, New Mexico
Shareholder

We would like to thank you and your Team for all the help and support you provided. You helped us start and operate our first dispensary, if it wasn't for Medbox we would not be where we are today. We are looking forward to opening many more locations with Medbox in 2014.
R. Doktorovich, Los Angeles and San Diego, California
Client

Medbox has been instrumental in not only helping us establish ourselves in the medical cannabis community, but they also continue to give us the confidence to move forward knowing they will be there to help navigate the incredibly grey areas of MMJ legislation successfully. More importantly they help to build your foundation on the most stable ground available, offering to light the path of least resistance in these still early "dark days" in the MMJ industry.

They have given our company the position, confidence and support to grow in this competitive thriving MMJ market. Being set up for success from day 1 allows us to focus on more important aspects of our business's growth. They offer long-term strategies for success and help to support you along the way at your pace.
M. Antonucci, Sherman Oaks, California
Client

It was important to me to set the record straight on our track record of successfully consulting with clients and helping them accomplish the goals they had hired us for. Despite the testimonials, however, the shorters didn't skip a beat and kept posting. That didn't matter to me, since anyone researching the company had clear and convincing proof that it was a real business and that we had happy clients and shareholders. It wasn't about proving the shorters wrong. They acted the way they did out of financial self-interest and would never see the light. It was more about giving the public the tools to make educated decisions on giving credence to the lies.

Medbox's stock price was stable, which obviously was no good for shorters. Organized shorting campaigns are a business that feeds and clothes these people and their children while other investors lose money in the stocks they target. Shorters are financial-market terrorists with little regard for others. After they found my pending criminal matter, they predicted that I would be convicted and go to jail. They relentlessly posted the same message a hundred different ways. I remained relatively calm and collected because I knew that the matter would soon be dismissed and later deleted from my record. Yes, we did have to make a public reference to the resolution of the criminal matter in the company's official filings, which we did within weeks of the case's conclusion. I always intended to communicate transparently about the company and its key people to the shareholders and public.

Near the end of 2013, Medbox's stock price was still trading in the twenty-dollar range, to the cheers of our shareholders and much to the chagrin of the shorters. The company had so far successfully fended off the organized short-and-distort campaign, but the shorters escalated by egging reporters on to write about me and my past. The reporters always contacted me and usually started off by saying they'd been tipped off. I always explained that the person contacting them was financially motivated. "Here's the real story…this is who I am." With that, the mainstream journalists understood the situation and didn't want to be a tool for the shorters to undermine the company's market. They were content with my explanations and left the matter alone.

On August 16, 2013, Roddy Boyd, a self-styled journalist, asked me for an interview. Boyd worked for what he called a nonprofit—the Southern Investigative Reporting Foundation (SIRF). During our talk, Boyd asked me to comment on statements I had allegedly made to him, but he had twisted my words. At that point, I demanded that all questions be tendered in writing so I could document everything we said. What he published was alarming. On September 30, his article was titled "Tinkerer, Lawyer, Hustler, Lies: One Man's Path to a Dope Fortune." It was an absolute mockery, primarily fiction made to look like fact. Boyd even took his mission to short-circuit Medbox's stock a step further and bought sponsored ad space at the top of our Yahoo Finance page with a link to his article. I was outraged and immediately had one of our attorneys, who was skilled in pursuing defamation claims, research Boyd and his prior activities.

What my attorney found was very telling but not at all surprising. That firm wrote an investigative memorandum for me with footnotes and citations. Some highlights are as follows:

Roddy Boyd is not the objective financial reporter he claims to be. Rather, he makes his living writing hatchet pieces designed to artificially depress the stock price of targeted public companies. He and his business associates (including his family members) then short sell the stock and make a tidy profit. Recently, Boyd set his sights on Medbox and its founder, Vincent Mehdizadeh. In evaluating information disseminated by Boyd (and his affiliates) regarding Medbox and/or Mehdizadeh, the hearer should keep the following in mind.

Boyd is closely connected to some of the major players engaged in these schemes, among them some of the biggest names on Wall Street. Moreover, Boyd has played a role in many of the lawsuits filed against these Wall Street firms and their principals alleging abusive short selling, including "short and distort" conspiracies.

One of Boyd's associates in the shorting community is the infamous shorter/distorter, Joe Carnes. In 2011 and 2012, several Chinese companies listed on the US stock exchanges brought lawsuits against an anonymous blogger or group of bloggers using the pseudonym "Alfred Little." Although not named in any of these lawsuits, Boyd wrote hit pieces on at least one of the Chinese companies in an apparent distortion scheme with Little. The suits alleged, among other things, that "Little" published false reports about the target companies through the website "Seeking Alpha" as part of a short sale market manipulation strategy. Jon Carnes has admitted that he was behind the Alfred Little financial blog. In December 2013, officials at the British Columbia Securities Commission—Canada's equivalent of the SEC—issued a press release accusing Carnes of massive investment fraud, including being the mastermind of one of the largest short and distort schemes in recent history.

Boyd's association with Wall Street's biggest short-sellers was likely facilitated by his family connections. Until 2011, Boyd's father, Michael Boyd, ran the hedge fund Forest Investment Management, LLC. Prior to founding Forest, Michael was a partner in Forum Capital Markets. Michael's co-founder in Forum was C. Keith Hartley, a disciple of Michael Milken—the "Junk Bond King," who pled guilty to securities fraud charges in 1989 and was sentenced to ten years in prison. Since then, Milken and his companies have entered the naked short selling game.

And Boyd's father has apparently given Roddy a large fortune. According to investigators, Boyd is the beneficiary of $30 million in trust funds affiliated with a Boyd Family Holdings LLC set up by his father.

SIRF

Boyd publishes many of his hit pieces on his SIRF website, which, again, he owns. SIRF's stated goal is to provide "in-depth financial investigative reporting for the common good." In reality, SIRF was established as a vehicle for Boyd's distortion efforts.

SIRF's list of donors reads as a veritable "Who's Who" in the world of short selling, and includes the Boyd Family Foundation, *established by Boyd's father as well as many others known for targeted shorting campaigns.*

Whether through his family ties, business associates, or friends, the inescapable and obvious reality is that Boyd has surrounded himself with individuals who make money when a company's stock price goes down.

Boyd and SIRF published the statements contained in his articles, and others like them, knowing that they were false and with the intention of harming Mehdizadeh and Medbox and manipulating Medbox's stock price. Mehdizadeh subsequently corrected Boyd and demanded that he remove his defamatory statements. Boyd refused, hiding behind laws that prohibit lawsuits against public participation.

Shortly after the Boyd incident, another shorter by the name of Andrew J. Left stepped into the Medbox spotlight. He is the editor for a blog called *Citron Research*. Unlike Boyd, Left publicly announces his short positions in the companies he targets. In his article "Busting Medbox," he cites Boyd's article and says that Medbox had "3 sets of accounting records," along with a host of other nonsensical and inflammatory statements. He even went as far as to challenge Medbox and specifically me to sue him if we felt his remarks were inaccurate. His brazen attitude even earned him a live interview on CNBC to discuss the "Medbox Fraud." I immediately countered his statements and issued the following press release to shareholders:

Medbox's Largest Shareholder Responds to Left's Criticisms
Dear Medbox Shareholders:
We are being attacked by a company called Citron Research, whose principal admits to making his living by short selling companies. Now, I have never made any allusions of having a blemish-free past myself and have been painfully honest in company filings in that regard, but I don't go around casting stones at others.

In my opinion, if you are going to take that approach and pick on others, you better have a spotless past yourself.

Here is some background on our opponent:

Citron Research is a one-man show run by Mr. Andrew Left, whose career began with a huge black mark. In 1998, in his first job, Mr. Left was found by the National Futures Association to have: "MADE FALSE AND MISLEADING STATEMENTS TO CHEAT, DEFRAUD OR DECEIVE A CUSTOMER IN VIOLATION OF NFA COMPLIANCE RULES 2–2(a) AND 2–29(a)(1)." Mr. Left was debarred for three years, among other punishments. This finding can be found on the website of the National Futures Association.

After being debarred, Mr. Left was employed as the President & CEO of Detour Media in 1999. But in February 2002, his company sued him for stealing six checks worth about $25,000. In Detour Media's official SEC filing, the company alleged Mr. Left's "fraud and deceit, negligent misrepresentation, breach of fiduciary duty and unlawful monetary conversion."

In 2005, Mr. Left founded stocklemon.com, a predecessor to citronresearch.com. On this website, he slammed a company called WHIS, and one of WHIS's principals, Mr. Salim Rana. He fabricated information about Mr. Rana (calling him a thief who steals from the elderly), and Mr. Rana sued Mr. Left for libel. The court issued a judgment, ordering Mr. Left to pay Mr. Rana $2,500,000 for damages. (Rana vs. Harris et al., Case No. BC313956, Default Judgment, Oct. 28, 2005, Cal. Super. Ct., Los Angeles County).

In 2010, Mr. Left again ran into trouble with the law, in an altercation with a businessman. He was arrested in Florida. In addition, the records show that he was charged for "failing to appear."

One has to wonder why an investor would trust the investment advice of someone with a record of fraud, deceit, and unlawful behavior. I'm conflicted on how to proceed as Left has made bold statements and is daring us to sue him. I am confident that the statements he has made are actionable but I have a personal goal of reducing the company's expenses and not wasting company funds on trivial pursuits. However, I don't mind going after him with personal funds and may pursue the same after I seek the advice of counsel on the matter. My colleagues at Medbox all have unblemished records and Mr. Left's comments as to a culture of civil and criminal disobedience by Medbox officers is patently false and unjustified. Similarly, his comments as to the company's unethical practices are untenable and completely unwarranted.

Thanks for all the support through the years. We are lucky to have fantastic shareholders.

Regards,

P. Vincent Mehdizadeh

While this type of shareholder communication is typically frowned upon in corporate America, unless companies and their principals speak up for themselves, if the only voice in the room is that of a liar, that's the one that gets heard. I couldn't afford to have Medbox fall victim to blatant attacks simply because the company was the beneficiary of a high share price. The company and its shareholders deserved to have a voice as well. With the release, the company weathered the storm. As for Andrew Left, I don't believe he ever appeared on CNBC again or any other news outlet, for that matter, after my press release on his less-than-ideal past.

The latter part of 2013 was incredibly eventful for Medbox. I had the idea to reward the shareholders that had helped the company achieve such epic success by issuing a bonus share for every common share they held. The extra share would only go to the common class of shareholders, boosting their equity, and was restricted from sale for about a year. Here is an excerpt from our press release on December 19, 2013:

Medbox Declares a 2-for-1 Stock Split in the Form of a Special Stock Dividend

Company rewards common shareholders with additional equity and voting power

Medbox, Inc. (OTC Markets: MDBX) (www.medboxinc.com), a leader in providing industry specific consulting services and patented systems to the medical and retail industries, announced a 2-for-1 stock split effected in the form of a common stock dividend. The 100% stock dividend issuance will have a record date of December 18th, 2013, a declaration date of December 28th, and a tentative issuance date of January 15th, 2014.

Management clarified that the class of shares to receive the dividend are the common shares only and not the preferred class of shares held by company executives.

"We wanted to reward existing shareholders and also increase the stock's marketability by making it attractive to a larger number of potential investors," stated Vincent Mehdizadeh, COO at Medbox, Inc. "The dividend results in a transfer of equity from company executives to our common shareholder base. I credit much of our company's breakout success to our loyal shareholders that believed in us in our early stages and have allowed us to expand at an enormous rate."

According to management, prior to the split, common shares held just under 50% of stockholder equity and voting power. After the split, common shares hold 2/3 of stockholder equity and voting power. The total issued and outstanding shares of common stock and preferred stock on a fully diluted basis, which was 29,500,750 will then be 44,500,750.

"What sets us apart from most other companies in our space is our low issued and outstanding share count, attention to transparency, relationship with our shareholders, and overall work ethic," stated Dr. Bruce Bedrick, CEO of Medbox, Inc. "We are going into a new year that has the makings of being our most exciting to date."

The company has been advised that under the Internal Revenue Code and the regulations thereunder as presently in effect, the receipt of one additional share for each share held on December 18th, 2013 will not constitute taxable income to shareholders for US Federal tax purposes. The company advises each shareholder to seek their own tax advice on how this stock dividend impacts them.

All shareholders, whether shares are held electronically or in paper form, will receive their shares from the company's transfer agent upon FINRA approval of the dividend, estimated at no later than January 15, 2014. The newly issued shares will be restricted from sale for 12 months, at most.

Within a few weeks of this announcement, the company's stock price again catapulted to epic levels, trading millions of shares worth hundreds of millions of dollars. By the end of trading on January 7, 2014, the share price sat at a whopping $73.10, making the company worth over $2.1 billion and my net worth about $1.4 billion. Over a year had passed since the initial spike in Medbox's stock price, and the company was not only keeping pace, but we were kicking ass! Around that time, I decided to sell a small amount of shares publicly every day, since I had not yet directly benefited from the company's tremendous success. I took my role as a founder very seriously and didn't want my sales to negatively impact the market for Medbox's stock.

During the latter part of 2013 and all throughout 2014, I publicly sold 62,000 shares of Medbox stock as well as 978,734 shares privately to accredited investors I had come to know. The stock in these private sales could not be resold for a year. This strategy took selling pressure off the stock and made sure our market was not negatively impacted by my sales. I could have legally sold these shares publicly, amassing a fortune well over $100 million after taxes, but this would undoubtedly have hurt the market for the company's stock and left existing shareholders with losses. In other words, I avoided consequences similar to those of a pump and dump.

Personal wealth had never been the be-all and end-all for me, because I had already lost everything once in my life and realized that money was really a means to an end and not the end itself. I was more focused on building something that would last, have value, and never lose relevancy. Cashing out would have meant that I didn't believe in my own company, and that was certainly not the way I felt or what I wanted to convey to the company's shareholders. All told, I had a small fortune at that point of about $6 million in cash. I lent some to Medbox on a low-interest loan and used the rest to buy my dream home. I was content with my success and happy to keep building Medbox's value for the shareholders, including me, the single largest shareholder.

Part of entrepreneurship is challenging yourself to be the best possible in all aspects of business and personal life. I started my philanthropic endeavors in the middle of 2013, by giving to St. Jude Children's Research Hospital and a variety of charities that focused on cannabis policy. I gave millions of dollars in stock and cash to them and felt good doing it. I also sponsored and participated in programs geared at educating patients and consumers in medical- and recreational-cannabis states. I named and personally sponsored the programs "Consume Responsibly" and "Medicate Responsibly," which were facilitated by the Marijuana Policy Project and Americans for Safe Access, respectively. I gave Medbox the credit for these campaigns and positioned the company's alternate mission as educating the public and always being "part of the solution" for the cannabis industry, never part of the problem.

CHAPTER 12

— ❧ —

Appointing a Board and Management Team and Being Shown the Door Like Steve Jobs at Apple, Circa 1985

<u>Entrepreneurs must carefully choose who they surround themselves with because one wrong hire can lead to utter chaos.</u>

I HAD A multifaceted focus in early 2014. I wanted to add talent to Medbox's board of directors and executive-management team, further the company's new business model (working with our successful dispensary and cultivation licensees to maximize efficiency), and position the company as the very first US-based cannabis-related company to achieve a NASDAQ listing. I felt that all of these goals were very much within reach.

Our first director appointment was Mitch Lowe in March of 2014. Mitch was an amazing find, as he had a ton of public-company experience and was the ex-president of Redbox and cofounder of Netflix. His big-business background made him an epic appointment to Medbox's board. In fact, it was the first time in history that a big-name executive had been appointed to a board of a cannabis-related public company. CNBC immediately picked up on the story and wanted a live interview with Mitch and Bruce, who was still serving as the company's CEO. Days after the announcement, there the two of them were, on live TV. It was yet another milestone for the company, and as I watched the interview at Medbox headquarters, I couldn't help but feel that I was indeed living a dream that most entrepreneurs never would experience. I was again humbled, but a sense of responsibility crept into me like a ghost invading my soul. This was all real, and I needed to make sure that the company never took its proverbial foot off the gas pedal. We had all the momentum, but we needed to do more and more to keep our shareholder value high and the company progressing toward NASDAQ.

Around that time, our CFO said that he felt we needed to move some of the company's booked revenue from 2012 to 2013; some work we had performed for Arizona contracts had been reported in the wrong year. This was because it had had to be delayed while the governor of Arizona temporarily halted the state's dispensary licensing program. Though our paperwork showed that the revenue was originally supposed to belong to 2012, some of it had to be done later. I was alarmed but thought that if the company had to declare the adjustment, it wouldn't be catastrophic for shareholder confidence. I advised Tom to do it correctly.

Over a million dollars in revenue was transferred from 2012 to 2013, and a press release was issued along with corrected financials. As a result, the company fielded some criticism—that's when Andrew Left made his "3 sets of books" accusation. But the company had done the right thing, and shareholder sentiment remained high in the first half of 2014.

In April, I took what I realized later was a meeting with the devil himself. Ned had been referred to Medbox by an interested party who said he had an ex–US ambassador who was interested in the cannabis industry and willing to join the board of directors. Bruce spoke with Ned and urged me to meet him in person to see if he was a fit for Medbox's board. Bruce said that someone with the political connections Ned claimed to have would be a big deal for us. In Las Vegas, Ned and I ate steak, drank a couple of cocktails, and chatted about Medbox's prospects. He was very charming. He said that he had been watching Medbox for some time and was impressed with my entrepreneurship and ability to overcome obstacles. I asked if he knew about my checkered past, and he replied, "I know all about you."

After we traded some questions, I thought he seemed like a good fit for Medbox. An ex–US ambassador sitting on a cannabis-related public company's board seemed like it would bring even more credibility and maintain the company's shareholder value. Thinking of my dreams to list the company on the NASDAQ by year's end, I offered Ned a seat on the board. It would prove to be the biggest mistake of my life.

Things began moving faster and faster toward mid-2014. The board had convinced me that it was time to transition out of management and act as consultant and founder. I actually had planned to do this anyway, since my director and officer roles allowed shorters to target me. I certainly didn't want to bring the company down. It was clear that the right move was to change roles. I ran through the plan with the board. I would return to Medbox's board once all criminal convictions had been expunged from my record, which my attorneys had told me I should be able to effect by 2016 with a petition to the court.

In the back of my mind, I was keenly aware of how corporate takeovers can occur from the inside and that a board can have less than an honorable agenda. But since I was the majority shareholder, I reasoned that the board served at my pleasure and that all big decisions affecting Medbox would have to go through me. As I transitioned out of management in mid-2014, company decision-makers, including me and Bruce, brought on Guy, who was a professional CEO with public-company experience, to run the company in Bruce's place. Though Bruce and I had done a great job, we had very little public-company experience and realized that Medbox needed experienced management to continue being viable and relevant. Bruce and I stayed on as consultants.

This didn't mean I worked less. I came into the office for the same sixty hours a week but focused my attention on making sure the company ran smoothly. I would still do all the little things that make a company successful, like answering clients and shareholders when needed, along with helping management in any way I could. To make the giant leap to NASDAQ, Medbox only needed a majority of independent directors on the board. I set out to recruit the third, looking first to industry-related charities to see if they had any leads on a high-profile director candidate.

Jennifer, a retired assistant director of the FBI's Security Division, would be a major coup for Medbox and the cannabis industry as a whole.

I explained to Jennifer our aspirations to be the best in the business and our focus on security and the compliance of dispensary operators through the use of our technology. I also explained that my past had been distorted in articles by financially motivated bloggers. I asked her to do her due diligence on me and Medbox. After some schmoozing by Ned and Mitch, she agreed to join the board. By July, I had accomplished everything I had wanted to do for the company that year. We had an amazing management team: Tom as CFO, Guy as CEO, Ned, and Mitch—and Jennifer about to be appointed. I had assembled a cast of all-stars.

With months to spare, I focused on strengthening the company's new business model. I noticed that Ned had been phasing me out of company discussions and wouldn't talk with me at all as he once had. His charming demeanor had turned cold, and he seemed distant and calculating. I chalked it up to him being busy. Later, I realized that as soon as I had confirmed the shareholder consent to appoint him to the board months after he had already joined us, his attitude toward me completely changed. Before I signed that all-important document for him, he stated that he wanted to be a mentor to me and relished in the opportunity to help me build Medbox into a force to be reckoned with for many years to come.

In retrospect, one conversation with him sticks out in my head that was both comical and spoke to his level of dysfunction. He told me once, "Vince, I love you." I jokingly responded, "Love me? You just met me!" Something seemed odd about that, but I rationalized that he really liked the company and was simply enamored of being in the position to help us achieve a higher level of greatness. He also knew that I had lost my mother tragically, and in the back of my mind, I thought he might be leveraging my troubled past to gain favor by acting like a father figure of sorts. He was already on the board at that point. I had some vague discussions with Bruce about whether Ned's motivations were genuine, but Bruce voiced his support for Ned, and I was reluctant to rock the boat. Things seemed to be generally on the right track.

In August of 2014, I received sobering news from Alex, the company's CPA. A federal grand jury had subpoenaed him for records related to me, my holding companies, and Medbox. Alex also was my personal and corporate CPA, so he had extensive records. While the news was shocking, I realized that the subpoenas were a result of Will's unsupported complaints to the SEC and FBI about my alleged criminal activities. I reasoned that government agencies were careless if they didn't at least investigate such concerns. I rested assured that nothing would turn up since I hadn't done what Will had alleged. I informed our board and corporate attorneys of the situation. We soon heard that our auditor had received an identical subpoena.

Things moved faster and faster over the next few months while we tried to figure out what was going on and why. Remember, too, that the company's auditor was also dealing with charges related to poor work. I felt that Tim's issue might very well have drawn more regulatory attention in concert with Will's complaint, but I remained confident that the issue would resolve itself. Shortly thereafter, Guy terminated Tom, the company's CFO. Doug, an alternate CFO, was installed. Ned had orchestrated Tom's removal by harassing Guy about it. I was privy to some of the conversations in which he had questioned Tom's work ethic. I felt it was unfair, but I wasn't in a position at that point to question management or the board about their decisions.

In late October 2014, I sat in on a board session as I commonly did at the time. The board said it was issuing a press release and filing a Form 8-K with the SEC (a material event summary) that would also be immediately available to the public. This action went against the advice of the company's SEC counsel, who had said that the inquiries we were under often resulted in no action being taken and that it was premature to announce anything. Ned led the charge to issue the statement, lobbying the rest of the board. Though I disagreed with the logic, the consensus was that the subpoenas needed to be made public. I asked to see the statement prior to release, but what came out on October 31, 2014, turned out to be quite different:

...(the "Company") appointed a special board committee, composed of all four of its current directors, that is, three independent directors and its recently appointed Chief Executive Officer/ Chairman of the Board, to investigate (i) a letter from a former Company employee to the Securities and Exchange Commission alleging wrongdoing by a former officer of the Company who is currently a consultant to the Company, and (ii) a federal grand jury document subpoena served in August 2014 on the Company's accountants by the US Department of Justice, to ascertain what implications, if any, the subpoena or the letter may have with respect to the Company.

The issue that I had was that there was no need for the company to point the finger at a "former officer of the Company who is currently a consultant." There were only three people in that demographic: Tom, Bruce, and I. And a disclosure of this magnitude should be accompanied by a press release giving the investment community some type of guidance to avoid investor panic and save the company's shareholders from losing a ton of value. In my management of Medbox over many years, I used commonsense principles in communicating to shareholders. I never held back information; I knew investors wanted to be leveled with and given all possible assurances from the board and management amid any controversy and speculation. Medbox's appointed decision-makers did not do this, which was a big mistake.

At the time the statement was released, I was on a flight to New York for a minivacation. As soon as I touched down, I immediately called Guy, our new CEO, and expressed my disappointment that an alternate version of the 8-K had gone out and without a press release to accompany it. He stated that I had seen a draft of the 8-K and that the board had the right to change it at any time. While I was upset, I understood that in corporate America, the board does what the board does.

I asked again about the lack of explanatory press release, which would have been standard operating procedure. There was a pause on the phone, and Guy sheepishly responded that "things could had been handled better." I kept my composure, since Guy had been my selection for CEO, and I certainly didn't want to burn a bridge with him. I asked if I could author such a press release now and have the board review it, and he agreed. Later, Mitch backed my idea. The board and management recognized me as a skilled communicator; I had authored most of Medbox's press releases to that point.

My November 3, 2014, release read as follows:

Medbox Comments on Recent 8-K Filing
Medbox, Inc., (OTCQB: MDBX), the leading licensing, infrastructure and security specialist, patented technology provider, and partner to the cannabis industry, commented on the recent 8-K filing discussing matters pertaining to a former employee of the company who filed an employment claim and sent a letter to certain government agencies asserting claims against the Company. The former employee subsequently lost the employment claim. However, the Company is now internally investigating the letter's contents to ascertain validity of the claims.

The 8-K references that the Board of Directors of Medbox, Inc. appointed a special board committee to investigate, review, and evaluate a letter involving the Company, sent in May 2014 to certain government agencies by a former employee of Medbox. Within the last few weeks, Medbox was awarded a judgment against this employee on his employment claims, which demanded $1.5 million in damages related to the Company's alleged wrongdoing. Prior to litigation of the employment claim, and after repeated settlement demands were made by the former employee and rebuffed by Medbox, the employment claim was filed and sent along with a letter to government agencies by the former employee, alleging wrongdoing by the company.

Mr. Vincent Mehdizadeh, Founder and Consultant to Medbox stated, "The former employee vowed to retaliate against the

Company in any way he could after his illegal cash demands of the company were ignored. It now appears that writing a letter to government agencies filled with factual inaccuracies and blatant falsehoods was the most effective way to facilitate that goal."

Current management commented that the Company has not found any indications that the subject matter contained in the letter is true concerning the conduct of prior officers of the company. However, the company's internal investigation on the matter is still in process. The Company also clarified that no subpoenas have been served on the Company, its current or former officers, or anyone affiliated to the Company.

Mr. Mehdizadeh added, "I painstakingly put together the best management team and Board of Directors in our sector for a reason, and in their judgment this voluntary disclosure is what good public companies that have nothing to hide should do. The company will continue to demonstrate to shareholders, the investment community, and all other public company participants in the cannabis sector, how a well-run and respectable public company should operate. Medbox has and will continue to be the gold-standard for accountability."

The release resulted in an immediate boost in investor confidence and sentiment regarding Medbox's stock, and the market held firm during that trading day. What happened then jars me, even as I write this almost exactly two years later. Guy called to ask if I had sent out the release, and I said I had. His response was stoic. He stated, "The board didn't want you sending that out, and we prepared another press release that is sitting in your inbox now." To my utter dismay, the release rehashed the language of the 8-K and offered no clarifications or any reasonable communication to the company's shareholders. In fact, a release went out stating that the prior one had been "unauthorized" by the company's board and went on to quote, verbatim, from the 8-K filing. I was devastated. My rapport with the board had officially been destroyed. As I would learn later, this was all a part of Ned's master plan.

In the days that followed, the company's share price took a beating, declining more than 25 percent—from $14.00 to $9.99 per share—as panic set in and investors rushed to sell. Then, sensing obvious internal issue at Medbox with the conflicting press releases, the SEC Enforcement Division sent us a formal investigation notification. I walked into Guy's office and set the letter down on his desk. I said, "Well, it's a good thing neither I nor the company have anything to hide."

By mid-November 2014, within days of the SEC letter, I had compiled every document they would want to see, along with supporting explanations and narratives. I immediately forwarded the packet to the board and management at Medbox. This was greeted with silence. They had stopped conferring with me about the SEC inquiry. I called Ned about it immediately. To my surprise, he took my call, because he had only been sporadically available to me over the last few months. He replied, "Don't worry, Vince; it will all be over soon." At first, I felt comforted, but later that night, I couldn't help but think that the devil himself had spoken with me just a few hours before. As I found out later, he had meant something altogether different.

CHAPTER 13

— ❦ —

Losing Almost Everything...Again

_The path to continued success is peppered
with land mines...one wrong step and your life
could be forever changed._

WHEN YOU BUILD something from nothing in business, you are proud, and you draw your identity from it. Taking into account the incredible value I had created for the shareholders of Medbox, including myself, my identification with the company was all encompassing. If things go sideways for the business, you lose a part of yourself along with it. I was deeply embroiled in the Medbox turmoil, which worsened as November 2014 went on. In fact, the board put me on hold as a consultant until further notice. Much of this was Ned's work for his own agenda, which was still not yet completely clear to me.

On December 1, 2014, I received yet another huge surprise and shock to the system. I had hired my own attorney to interface with the Medbox board's attorney, professionalizing my communications with the company's new management for understandable reasons. My attorney told me that Medbox's board had decided to restate financials for the company's prior two years of operations and possibly even more. The numbers being discussed were in the hundreds of thousands or possibly millions of dollars in revenue being wiped off the books as if it had never occurred. I was stunned.

The way I saw it, Medbox had been my "baby" that I had eventually sent to a prestigious Ivy League university (my handpicked board and management team) to groom it for a successful adulthood (NASDAQ listing). Now, the university had decided that my child needed a lobotomy and would have a better life as a vegetable on life support while they filled their coffers with Ivy League tuition in perpetuity. That kind of re-statement of financials makes prior management (and their accounting professionals) look incompetent. It decimates shareholder sentiment, fuels panic in the market for the company stock, makes the company look like an absolute sham, and tarnishes the reputations of everyone associated with the company during the period in question. This is like a third party petitioning a court for custody of a child—the method is to make the parents look incompetent.

The kicker is that the board had made this critical decision without conferring with the company's prior CFO (Tom), the prior CEO (Bruce), or me, the prior COO. We all had intimate knowledge of every transaction since the company's beginnings. It was all too much to even fathom or comprehend. The company's new management didn't even inform the company's auditor or prior CFO that it was announcing a restatement.

On December 2, 2014, I e-mailed the following plea to the board and management at Medbox, copying Tom and Bruce:

> I am informed an 8-k is about to be issued that will cripple the stock and company irreparably. This 8-k calls into question 2013 revenues. Before the board takes this kind of action it would be necessary, not prudent, but necessary, for current management to communicate with prior management (Tom, Bruce, and I) to clearly understand all items of concern.
>
> This action you are taking will destroy the company and cripple our shareholders. Do not do this without having all the facts! Let's have a call to discuss this immediately before any public statements are made.

The same day, the attorney representing the board responded:

> Doug Mitchell, the current CFO, had a discussion with Tom about these issues on November 26.

To this, Tom responded as follows:

> Doug (Current CFO) asked me about San Diego (revenue for the company) in Q1-2013 and I explained the thought process on why the company justified the recognizing of revenue for the work done on the approx. 20 contracts. I also mentioned that the money back guarantee existed and it was brought to the attention of the SEC counsel at the time Penny Somer who heard my feelings on the matter and decided it didn't have to be disclosed. I also mentioned that there was an SEC comment letter on the subject that we responded to and that was the last I heard of it as we reversed the revenue for the change in the law that occurred in feb/march 2014 and fully disclosed the reasons in the 10Qs which are very detailed in 2014.
>
> It was never even hinted that there is a major restatement issue involved here.
>
> I do not know anything that transpired other than disclosed here but the need to restate is something that requires more in depth discussions than what I have been privy too.
>
> Restatements involve materiality and how an investor would be swayed by the publication of the incorrect information. One of the things positive for Medbox is the publicity of the industry and Medbox TV time are the largest swayer of the stock not the reported financial results. The historical stock price graphs will help show that.
>
> I would be happy to discuss the details with people if needed but my understanding is that the SEC hadn't had any further comments and accepted our disclosures on the san diego matter and moved on.

I was having a good day until this popped up.

I am happy to help but unless there is some overriding new information that I don't know about (which could be a lot) I would be very hesitant to restate things again.

Tom

Based on the "new information" the board had received, they agreed to delay the public filing concerning the restatement and the 8-K announcement and investigate the matter further. As if the restatement issue weren't enough, there was yet another problem: an S-1 registration statement filed with the SEC months earlier was to go into effect immediately, resulting in millions of dollars of funding from a group of investors and lenders in exchange for shares at a favorable price. We had worked on raising this capital for months, and now the much-needed funding was to arrive. In the recent e-mail thread, it became clear that the company's board intended to pull the plug on the S-1, canceling the capital infusion just when the company needed it.

I sent an e-mail that read as follows:

Doing so will hurt the company with the lenders that loaned the company money and were told that effectiveness was eminent on December 3. The company is about to yet again send out huge red flags to regulatory authorities, shareholders, our lenders, and the investment community that things are not ok. As we learned today the current CFO failed in properly assessing the situation and the company almost filed an 8-k that would have been the equivalent of doomsday. According to our current SEC counsel, "thanks for saving the day Vince, that 8-k would have meant a flurry of class action lawsuits and then an inevitable Bankruptcy being filed by Medbox." Furthermore, our auditor needs to be made aware of any 8-k regarding his work for the company and he was not made aware. What would have happened is he would have hit the roof, resigned, and publicly disagreed with the company's assessment. We stopped all this from happening today... Thank goodness.

What it is doing is causing me to reassess the situation at Medbox. I've blindly put faith in current management and a day like today makes me question the decisions management is making and how matters are being presented to the board. Doug (current CFO) is not right for an emerging growth company of this type. I respect his business acumen but it's just not a right fit. I've excluded him from this email as a courtesy.

The Medbox "investigation" into whether or not to issue restatements was a farce. The board and management asked me to come into the office on December 3, 2014, and review the financials with Guy and Doug. After about two hours of back and forth, where I brought things to the new CFO's attention that he should have known (or, if he didn't, should have asked the people who did), I realized that things were in a dire state at Medbox. The reality was that the new CFO, Doug, had made a decision on matters and reversing course meant he was wrong. This made for an impossible situation to overcome. How could Doug now come back to the board with his tail between his legs and tell them he was wrong about the restatement being necessary? The simple answer was, he couldn't.

I realized later that the situation had been by Ned's design completely. He was the one who had replaced Tom, planning it months before any subpoenas. He was the one who had told me that anytime there was a change of CEO at a public company, it also customarily changed its CFO—which I later found out was not accurate. In fact, much of what Ned told me was self-serving and meant to fit his specific agenda. My realization that Doug couldn't reverse course on the restatements even if he had wanted to, which I believe he did, became even clearer when Guy told me that the company was actually deregistering the S-1 shares. It was "a board decision." I believe it was mainly Ned's.

So, our new funding had been terminated. The board's decision had made my time at the office meaningless and Doug changing course impossible. I left, telling Doug and Guy that I was discouraged by their performance, and, as the majority shareholder of the company, I would weigh my options for a management change. That day, I sent the Medbox board the following e-mail:

Dear Jennifer, Mitch, and Ned:

Let me start off by saying that I am 100% confident that the relationship between our independent directors and the majority shareholders of Medbox (Bruce and I), can prosper and become better over time. I do not feel the situation has reached a point where it cannot be repaired between us. Both the businessman and good person in me knows that to be true.

That being said, current management is another story. Bruce and I have started discussions about that particular issue and are continuing discussions on Friday. Although I do possess the ability to impose my will on this company, through a written consent action as allowed for in the company by-laws, articles, and by Nevada Statute (state of incorporation), I am not going to act in that capacity unilaterally which is why I am discussing matters with Bruce, and our attorneys, on Friday. Bruce shares my concerns about current management.

Terminating Guy Marsala and Doug Mitchell for cause is the right thing to do for several reasons:

Doug Mitchell prepared and presented to the board an incomplete report regarding Q3 2013 revenues and didn't even know where to look for the documentation in the office. I had a 2 hour meeting today with him and Guy which resulted in both of them conceding they had mischaracterized the situation. Why that is especially important is that I hopped into action yesterday after learning of this erroneous 8-k about to be filed and cooler heads prevailed and the document was not filed. This is the cause needed to terminate both Doug and Guy without severance.

Additionally, Doug and Guy failed to notify our Auditor that a restatement was coming. He was absolutely livid when our former CFO called him and told him the news, only after I informed our former CFO of the same. The contract with our Auditor requires the company to notify him of anything remotely close to this magnitude and management failed to do so.

The office is at an absolute standstill according to other employees on the job that I spoke with today. Nothing is getting done and Guy has had his door closed for weeks on end. No one feels any leadership from him on the job. All this and the restatement calamity caused me to tell him that I would be reporting back to work starting Friday as a consultant to the company. He stated, "no you will not." To which I stated that I would be reaching out to the board to terminate him and Doug for cause.

To reiterate, Bruce and I respect a board of this caliber immensely and do not want to uproot the board in any way. Both of us take pride that we were able to attract the talent serving on our board. So please take this email for what it is, a majority shareholder reaching out to the company's board for help. In the interim, and until we find a new CEO, Matt Feinstein has agreed to step in as interim CEO and Board Chairman. I have also reached out to Tom Iwanski and despite the rude way he was terminated by Guy, he *has stated he will help in his old capacity with the company until we find a more permanent CFO. I would also like to recommend Eric K******, whom is a very skilled Attorney to serve as an additional director so we can round out the board at 5.*

These are my recommendations and I will have further comments after discussing the matter with Bruce and attorneys on Friday.

Feel free to write back if you have questions concerning the foregoing.

The board didn't respond, and through my attorney, I heard that they intended not to. The action it took was meant to demoralize me and destroy any semblance of continuity or morale for the supporting cast: Medbox's employees. It (Ned) hired armed guards to keep me out of Medbox headquarters. I had to wonder whether the board knew what it was doing. Ned had carefully planned all the maneuvers to undermine my authority and set the company on a course of his choosing.

The next day, December 4, 2014, I sent the following e-mail:

Guy and Doug:

By terminating the registration statement that went effective today you have put the company into financial ruin. The company was set to collect $2.5m from its lenders based on the effectiveness of this registration statement and now the company can't collect and is in default on the initial notes to those lenders. Management has put the company on a course for bankruptcy. I have executed a written consent action effective December 3rd removing the incumbent directors from the corporation. Hopefully I can undo the damage you have done with your extra conservative and nonsensical approach. News flash, the company cannot survive this way. It is going to be my position that the *directors did not have authority to make this decision when it was made today.*

Executed Written Consent Action effective December 3 along with termination notices for Doug and Guy forthcoming.

Regards,

Vincent Mehdizadeh

I then e-mailed to the Medbox board:

Attached please find written consents for the removal and appointment of the new board. Ned, Mitch, and Jennifer, you are welcome to engage in a dialogue with me should you wish to be re-appointed on to the new board.

Guy and Doug, please take this as formal notice that you are terminated as officers and directors of any and all Medbox companies, with cause, effective immediately. Please take your security guard that was hired to keep me off premises with you.

Regards,

Vincent Mehdizadeh

I couldn't remove management, even though I was majority shareholder, without first removing the board of directors. It was a move that I didn't want to make, but the board had forced my hand. I'm sure that Ned reassured the board to stay confident in Medbox management and refuse to even respond to my pleas to reshuffle the deck at headquarters. I offered current board members the opportunity to rejoin after I appointed others to balance out the decision-making process, to demonstrate that I simply wanted additional oversight at the board level, not to undermine their authority or embarrass them professionally. I appreciated their business prowess, but I couldn't stand idle while they blew critical decisions. In addition, none of them had any cannabis-industry experience and were costing the company millions of dollars in stock compensation per quarter. The compensation was way too high. Ned had facilitated the compensation for himself and the other board members to the detriment of the company and its shareholders.

Following my e-mails, Medbox's attorney contacted mine, who advised me to try to work with the existing board since replacing them during an SEC investigation might look like obstruction and that I had something to hide. I was again shocked. This was exactly what Ned had been looking to accomplish: ostracize the founder and majority shareholder, make prior management look incompetent, make it harder for the majority shareholder to seize control because of the active SEC investigation, and gain control of the company.

Tom said to me at one point that he felt Ned had always been after control of the company and that he was a "snake in the grass." Now I needed to strategize how to get rid of the snake without it biting me and sending me to my grave. I had been playing chess with a formidable opponent without even knowing it. The call I had had with Ned weeks earlier replayed in my head: "Don't worry, Vince; it will all be over soon." I settled down and realized I would need a cool head to match wits with him.

I sent this e-mail later that day:

To the Board:

At present, I am holding off on formally serving the written consent actions I distributed earlier today, but reserve the right to serve the same at some point in the future. I do not condone of how Doug and Guy have handled themselves as they have failed the company in a myriad of ways. I will closely monitor the situation and I suggest the board step in and find replacements immediately. Furthermore, I'm electing to come back from hiatus starting December 15th, 2014. The company desperately needs my input so please terminate Doug and Guy prior to that date. I recommend Matt be the interim CEO until a suitable replacement can be found, and Tom Iwanski can step back into his role until a permanent solution can be found at CFO. I have faith in both.

Thank you,
Vincent Mehdizadeh

I expected a new, healthy dialogue with the board to get the company on the path to recovery. I received a single response: Ned simply copied everyone on my original e-mail and said, "Vince blinked again." He was attempting to rattle me, saying that I had backed down. It confirmed my beliefs about Ned's malevolent intentions and destructive behavior at Medbox.

The board's attorney apologized for Ned's comment, and my attorney sent an e-mail directed at Ned:

I feel compelled to respond to your flippant and inflammatory comment by advising you that Vince is obviously more reflective and thoughtful than the "chicken littles" running amok with limited information who make "knee-jerk" reactions and decisions that would have serious and possibly irreparable consequences for a company you are only recently involved in. I suggest you keep your belligerent comments to yourself and focus on your obligations to the company and its legitimate shareholders!

I mistakenly thought that after Ned had showed his authentic self, the board might actually operate more independently from him, but that was wishful thinking on my part. The board seemed to want to help Ned carry out his master plan. I got legal advice on how to remove the board of directors, regardless of how the SEC might view the management and board shake-up.

The next few weeks were some of the oddest of my life, and given what I had been through to date, that was saying quite a lot. The employees at Medbox, who were overwhelmingly loyal to me, told me that the board and management continued to maintain their three security guards. Then, five days before Christmas 2014, Ned and the board fired almost the entire staff without any explanation in a Friday-night e-mail. They were not to return to the office, and their personal effects would be mailed to them. It was devastating. I had known these people for years. They were good, honest, and ethical employees who didn't deserve to be treated like garbage simply because they were loyal to me. Ned and the board also terminated all SEC-attorney relationships the company had, replacing them with the firm the board was already using. My attorneys noted that this was an obvious conflict of interest and wondered who was looking out for the company and its shareholders.

The self-sabotage continued at Medbox. A December 30, 2014, press release announced it had "received subpoenas from the federal grand jury." I'm a big fan of full disclosure in business. However, the disclosure was inaccurate. A subpoena had never been issued to the company itself but to the company's accountants—months earlier and already reported to the public! What's worse, none of Medbox's leaders or attorneys caught the error. I figured that either those in charge at Medbox were incompetent, or Ned was sabotaging the company on purpose. I leaned toward the latter, which I immediately brought up to the new SEC attorney. Though my attorney received an apology for the error, no clarifying press release went out to the public. In fact, the erroneous press release reminded the public about the company's disastrous financial restatement.

The same day, I wrote a press release to the company's shareholders:

Dear Medbox Shareholders:

It has truly been an interesting journey during the last 2 years. When I commenced operations of the private company in 2010 that later became Medbox, I never anticipated that the company would be as noteworthy and relevant as we are today. The company has a rare blend of consulting and patented technology that gives entrepreneurs a jumpstart on realizing their dreams of operating a business in a newly emerging industry. I have thoroughly enjoyed watching our client's dreams be realized, along with our shareholders that have watched our company grow and prosper over these years.

Medbox rocketed to stardom and notoriety amidst a positive outlook for the cannabis industry in November of 2012 based on favorable election results and highlighted by several media sources, including the Wall Street Journal, which ushered in what many have called the "Green Rush." In the days that followed, the company's stock price saw unprecedented increases that was said to have resulted from investors looking to participate in "The Next Great American Industry." Up until 3 months ago, I was involved in almost every decision the company made, and my decision at that time was to caution investors about investing in any company in the cannabis industry because of the inherent risks. We also publicly cautioned investors to temper their expectations about our stock and to make informed investment decisions. The company fielded criticism in doing so, but we felt that separating ourselves from other public company industry participants in our sector and focusing on protecting investors as best we could was a beneficial direction for the company. In my opinion, one of the keys to Medbox's success has been superior corporate messaging and timely dissemination of information to our shareholders.

Since that point in time a little over two years ago, I have made it my mission to take the company from being a non-reporting pinksheet to being a fully reporting SEC Filer. I took it upon *myself to set these goals and achieve them for the benefit of the company and its shareholders. We did this to have an increased level of transparency so that investors can think of Medbox as the public company standard for respectability and reliability in the newly emerging cannabis industry that was taking shape. As a result, we engaged a Public Company Accounting and Oversight Board (PCAOB) registered auditor, Q Accountancy Corporation, and also hired a full-time Chief Financial Officer, Thomas Iwanski, a CPA with excellent references and extensive public company experience.*

Since the company engaged Mr. Iwanski and Q Accountancy Corporation, I also recruited a star-studded board and together we appointed Guy Marsala to lead the company as the Chief Executive Officer. As it was explained to me, in situations where a new CEO is brought on, they typically look to appoint their own Chief Financial Officer. Thus, when Mr. Marsala decided to replace Mr. Iwanski as CFO, I did not give it a second thought, although I was sad to see him go since his experience with public company oversight was superb.

Today, the company's current management issued a statement regarding the company's financials. Prior management, including Mr. Iwanski and the company's current auditor, both disagree with current management's position on the matter. Both the current auditor and prior CFO have made their opinions known to current management, to no avail. Both have stated that they had support for recognizing revenue in the periods in which they were recognized. However, the company's current CFO has a difference of opinion on that aspect and believes that the revenue in question should be recognized in later periods, which has now resulted in a proposed restatement set to occur. This fact along with the fact that the revenue items in dispute amount to less than 10% of the total revenue booked for 2013, was not accurately discussed in the disclosure released this morning.

As stated previously in this letter, corporate messaging and communication to shareholders is one of the many aspects that made Medbox a great company. I now feel the company is not doing enough to accurately disclose matters in a manner that is easy to understand and digest by the public. Stating that the current CFO has a difference of opinion with the prior CFO and current auditor would have gone a long way to explaining the situation properly. Instead, we have the inaccurate and incomplete disclosure that was released today that leaves the public with more questions than giving them the answers they need to understand the situation.

As we were on a path to transition to NASDAQ and had filed an application to be listed on that exchange, I felt that since I had a checkered past that was disclosed in company filings it would tarnish the Medbox brand if I stayed involved in any capacity other than as a consultant to the company. Although these offenses were non-violent, non-securities related offenses, all of which resulted in probation and all occurring prior to Medbox, I still felt that the company would always be a target of "short and distort" campaigns by financial bloggers if I remained an Officer or Director. To that end, I recently gave full control to the board and current management to steer the ship and navigate the company properly. Recent events have caused me to call into question whether current management and the board of directors has enough industry experience to properly run this company. It is for this reason that I will be adding industry-experienced members to the board to work with the current board members to more effectively operate the company. I will also be taking a more active role with the company again to ensure our short-term and long-term goals can be achieved.

I believe that a founder's passion separates a typical company from a company that achieves the utmost success. The company needs my help now more than ever, and I intend to fill that need to the best of my ability going forward. I look forward to a strong and prosperous future for Medbox.

Regards,
P. Vincent Mehdizadeh

Remarkably, amid all the restatement talk, botched investigation announcements, a phantom grand-jury subpoena, the canceled millions in capital, and obvious internal conflicts, company shares were still trading at over six dollars to end 2014. I had about twenty-eight million shares with substantial market support, and the company and I were still worth hundreds of millions of dollars. I had the power to turn things around. The shareholders of Medbox deserved better, and I was determined to right the ship.

Into the first week of 2015, I had been busy assembling a trustworthy management team and board of extremely talented and well-versed people. I had also quickly sourced a board-advisory committee of seasoned talent. On January 9, 2015, I filed my written-consent action with the SEC and issued this press release:

P. Vincent Mehdizadeh—Founder and Majority Shareholder of Medbox, Inc. (OTCQB: MDBX) filed a written consent action with the Securities and Exchange Commission that added 4 new directors with key industry experience in the disciplines of consulting, technology, and security. In addition, the company unveiled its Board Advisory Committee.

"We are taking the company back to what made us successful in the first place, keeping a lean budget, capitalizing on our industry best patents, targeting key endeavors, communicating

with shareholders, and being able to react quickly to regulatory changes as new opportunities present themselves," stated Vincent Mehdizadeh, Founder and Majority Shareholder, at Medbox. "The action taken today will allow the company the freedom to operate again with all hands on deck." Mehdizadeh clarified that the prior independent board members have all been asked to return, at their discretion, either on the board of directors at their regular salaries or on the board advisory committee at a far reduced fee. The existing CEO and CFO, Guy Marsala and Doug Mitchell, have been asked to return as consultants to the company to make the transition as seamless as possible. The company's former Vice-President, Matthew Feinstein, shall be interim President until a replacement can be sourced. Feinstein will then return to his role as Vice-President.

"We spent millions last year in director and officer compensation and while their impressive backgrounds in combination with the risk factors inherent to the industry we operate in might warrant such compensation, the company is better off reducing overhead and making a push this year to get profitable again. We have one newly elected independent director at present and have confirmed at least another independent joining the company by the end of January along with any of the prior independent directors looking to return to the company in that capacity."

The new look board is as follows:

Matthew Feinstein

Matthew Feinstein began consulting for Medbox in June 2013, and was promoted to Vice President in February 2014. He also served as a director of the Company from April 2014 until October

2014. Mr. Feinstein was Operational Supervisor at Redbox from 2009 until 2011. He was subsequently recruited to become Director of Operations at minuteKEY, a self-service key duplicating kiosk company from 2011 to 2012. Mr. Feinstein earned an undergraduate degree in Political Science at the University of California, Berkeley.

David Trecek

Mr. Trecek is a thirteen-year veteran of the security & surveillance industry. He is a seasoned C-Level manager who has designed and deployed enterprise class video surveillance systems for various national gaming providers such as Mandalay Bay, Bellagio, Harrah's, Lakes Entertainment, and multiple Native American tribes. He also managed the contract to deploy smaller footprint systems for the YUM! Brands portfolio: (KFC, Pizza Hut, Taco Bell) and their respective franchisees. Mr. Trecek is well versed in the areas of video surveillance, access control, alarm monitoring, remote video, voice, data and telecom.

Jaime Ortega

Jaime Ortega first started with the Company in 2010 during its early stages of corporate development. He was the Company's Field Service Manager overseeing day-to-day operations for Medbox machine maintenance and point-of-sale software updates with the company's information technology developer. Mr. Ortega has over 10 years' experience with computer repair, networking and software feature implementation. He helped to establish every Medbox dispensary location, as well as train employees and operators on key industry insight and knowledge.

P. Vincent Mehdizadeh

P. Vincent Mehdizadeh founded Medbox's main subsidiary, Medicine Dispensing Systems, in February 2008. He commenced operations for that company in 2010, and in December of 2011 sold that company to what became Medbox, Inc. Mr. Mehdizadeh served as senior consultant from December 2012 until May 10, 2013 for Medbox, Inc. and then transitioned to Chief Operations Officer and Board Chairman for Medbox, Inc. through May of 2014. Mr. Mehdizadeh was responsible for creating the 2 main patents behind the company's technology, helping to assemble the talented management team at Medbox, and also developing the concept behind the business models driving revenue for the company.

"The newly elected board is serving at a fraction of what was being paid to our prior board. I feel we have also added key industry experience and knowledge where it is needed most, on the board," stated Matthew Feinstein. "In addition, we have a fantastic Board Advisory Committee that we feel will help us improve as a company."

The Board Advisory Committee consists of a tax/financial expert, cannabis industry experts, a retired police chief, and a pharmacy industry expert. Their background and relevant experience is listed as follows:

Mario Cerreto, CPA

A graduate from the University of California Santa Cruz, Mario has over 6 years professional experience. Mario launched his career in accounting with Price Waterhouse & Coopers, LLP an international professional services Firm. There he led financial statement audits and reviews of publicly traded companies, developed and implemented key internal control procedures, and acquired technical accounting exposure to IPOs, debt restructuring, and revenue recognition projects. Mario transitioned to an Internal Audit role within the largest Non-Profit Healthcare Organization in Southern California, where he acquired significant experience in business process analysis and compliance. Then Mario joined a boutique accounting Firm in San Diego where he specialized in consulting and tax planning for small businesses and individuals, including Medical Cannabis dispensaries. Mario then established New Era CPAs, a full service Firm dedicated to the medical cannabis community. Mario specializes in include strategic tax planning and compliance projects while managing the day to day operations of the Firm.

Dr. Robert Melamede, Scientist and Industry Expert

Dr. Melamede has a Ph.D. in Molecular Biology and Biochemistry from the City University of New York. He retired as Chairman of the Biology Department at University of Colorado, Colorado Springs in 2005, where he continues to teach. Dr. Melamede is recognized as a leading authority on the therapeutic uses of cannabinoids, and has authored or co-authored dozens of papers on a wide variety of scientific subjects. Dr. Melamede also serves on the Scientific Advisory Board of Americans for Safe Access, the Unconventional Foundation for Autism, The World Aids Institute, Board Tim Brown Foundation (The Berlin Patient), Phoenix Tears Foundation, and regularly consults with professional and laypersons around the world regarding cannabis and health issues. He also served as a director of Newellink Inc, a Colorado-based company specializing in cancer research.

Edward M. Merrick, Jr., Retired Police Chief

Mr. Merrick has a distinguished 39 year law enforcement career and is a retired Chief of Police for the City of Plainville Massachusetts. Mr. Merrick rounds out the committee and is Instrumental in developing security protocols in all phases and components of a medical cannabis dispensary operation; including physical perimeter and interior security for grow and dispensary operations, product security to prevent theft or diversion and transportation and delivery security protocols.

Luke Kleyn, R.Ph. Chief Operating Officer—KMR Pharmacy Advisors

Mr. Kleyn is a Registered Pharmacist with more than 36 years of leadership experience in the pharmacy industry. He is known, in the marketplace, for developing innovative strategies to optimize growth, financial outcomes and improved operations while mitigating risk. He was Regional Vice President of PBM Sales & Service and Vice President of Clinics for the Walgreen Company. Mr. Kleyn was the primary architect for Walgreen's 90-Day Retail strategy and was responsible for many emerging strategies including the launch of On-Site Pharmacies at Medical Centers & Specialty Clinics and the launch of Walgreen's Take Care Clinics (now Healthcare Clinics). Currently, Mr. Kleyn is the Chief Operating Officer with KMR Pharmacy Advisors. KMR provides independent pharmacy consulting, with specific focus on all aspects of pharmacy, for Retail Pharmacies, Hospitals, Medical Centers, PBM's and Managed Care Organizations. He has developed highly customized solutions for his clients and understands the unique complexities inherent with the growth, financial, operational and risk management related to pharmacy. Mr. Kleyn has agreed to join the Medbox Board of Directors and will be appointed as an independent director in late January.

Mehdizadeh also addressed the proposed restatement set into motion by current management referenced in the company's 8-K of December 30, 2014. He stated, "We will be evaluating the impact of the proposed $403,000 of revenue being shifted from 2013 to the first 2 quarters of 2014 by hiring a qualified 3rd party accounting firm that will have the benefit of having all available information prior to making any conclusions as to whether, in their professional opinion, restatements should occur based on GAAP, relevancy, and materiality. New management will then communicate the findings to the shareholders and either restate or confirm prior financials accordingly. We believe this is the most proficient route based on the fact that the company's prior CFO and current auditor have disagreed with management's position on the matter and have stated that revenue was recognized correctly."

I had sourced a new board, management team, and board advisors. I had also invited the existing board back if its members wanted to continue to serve the company. Or they could walk away from a difficult situation with their heads held high. The written-consent action was set to take effect at the end of January 2015 to allow Medbox shareholders time to digest the notice of the changes, per SEC regulations. The action was a surprise to Ned and the board—my chess move aimed at saving the company. Ned thought he had had me sufficiently pacified, but I had a lot of fight left in me. There was simply too much at stake for the shareholders, and my legacy had become more and more tarnished. Something needed to happen.

On January 16, 2015, the board filed a lawsuit against me, alleging that I had taken advantage of the company and its shareholders. This ridiculous farce didn't give any examples of what I had done but stated generally that I had deceived the public and mismanaged Medbox affairs when I was in control of it. A fair number of its pages discussed the experience and high pedigree of the board and management team, leaving out that I had actually recruited and appointed them. A single paragraph followed about how I had committed various acts against the company and its shareholders. It was as vague as possible, but the rationale behind the complaint was abundantly clear—to discredit me and paint me as a "bad actor" for regulators watching the Medbox spectacle unfold.

All of the recent announcements and disclosures had prompted over twenty law firms to solicit Medbox shareholders as potential clients in class actions. They issued press releases linked to financial reporting websites where Medbox shareholders would see them. It was an absolute nightmare. It was every bit the circus Ned had been counting on. The one thing he hadn't counted on was that the lawsuits named him and the rest of the board as well as past and present management. Ned had thought he could wreak havoc on the company and that, meanwhile, he and the board would be spared as the heroes who had uncovered purported wrongdoing. But my public statements that revealed internal conflicts over the Medbox's direction had prevented that.

I realized that when it filed its suit, there was no way of working with the board because Ned controlled it and had a private agenda. I knew now that the board would not take any action to protect the shareholders. My attorneys were dumbfounded. None of them could figure out why the board was fighting so hard to usurp control of a company that was being sued and was embroiled in an investigation when its founder was ready, willing, and able to step in and lead it. But my attorneys failed to see what I had: Ned didn't care about the company's *current* reputation or shareholders. He didn't care if Medbox got ripped to shreds as long as he could rebuild the company himself after what he hoped would be a minor collapse. Medbox's market was still powerful, even in the current circumstances. Ned wanted to take control from me, the rightful leader, push the share price down and buy up the stock cheaply in the public market, and then resurrect the company under his own name, profiting on a rebound in the share price. He would receive credit for one of the most tremendous business turnarounds in recent history. Sound farfetched? Stay tuned.

While the lawsuit was disheartening and deflated my morale from a public-perception standpoint, I had more pressing and inescapable issues. The SEC investigation into Medbox was in full swing, and my attorneys felt that the Ned-led board was doing its best to push the investigation and regulators in my direction. The board members had big-business, government, and political backgrounds while I was the one with the checkered past. It made me an easy target and scapegoat of whatever story Ned cooked up.

And, since I was publicly trying to replace the Ned-led board, though my statements were never derogatory, the days following the lawsuit became a game of chicken between the board and me. It wanted me to withdraw the written-consent action before it went effective at the end of the month, using the lawsuit as leverage. The company's attorney offered to dismiss it if I agreed. However, the SEC had scheduled investigatory interviews with each of us for late January, so it watched the company's board and me publicly maneuver for control of Medbox. The SEC would interview the board just a few days before talking with me.

My attorneys became anxious about what could happen at the board's SEC interview. They had watched Ned maneuver like a snake for weeks and had little respect for him. They knew he was capable of just about anything. When someone has no morals, it can be dangerous to cross that person's path. The lawsuit had been a well-timed attack on my written-consent action and the forced exodus of the current board. They knew that my attorneys would advise me to withdraw the action with the other things going on. It was an untenable situation. I didn't want the mutually assured destruction we were headed for if I created a public battle against the board. The company, its shareholders, and I would all suffer. Ned guessed right, and he won that round. (Since I'd had no idea we were competing, I suppose he won all the previous rounds as well.)

Weighing all my options and the possible outcome of being directly at odds with the board, I withdrew the written-consent action, and Medbox's board agreed to dismiss its lawsuit. My attorneys noted that this gave the distinct impression that the lawsuit had never had merit. This was one of the reasons I had agreed to the compromise. The board had slung undeserved dirt on me, and I wanted to sling some much-deserved dirt back. If I kept the board in power, how did they intend to address the wrongs I had purportedly committed? Ned had spun his web of lies about me, and now he and the board would have to justify their dismissal of a lawsuit for my offenses against the company and its shareholders. That also goes for the interview with the SEC. It's hard to throw a guy under the bus with whom you just publicly compromised. "We filed the lawsuit because he was trying to replace us" doesn't convey solid corporate governance, ethical public-company management, or even morality. It speaks of people who would do anything to win. Ned is one of them, while I am proud to say that I am not. So, with that outcome, control of the company I founded was forever in the hands of someone I despise.

My attorneys continued to give me bits of news, and sometimes I attended conference calls for updates, as prenegotiated. Ned spent no time in clearing house once again at Medbox, in early 2015. In the first quarter, he appointed himself chairman of the board and constructively fired Guy, the CEO whom he had had a hand in recruiting. From what I gathered, Guy had caught on to Ned, who began having trouble controlling him. The company went months without informing the public of the open CEO seat and that Ned was actually running the show. They did this by keeping Guy on payroll for most of 2015 at $30,000 per month. He sat on the sidelines and appeared by telephone, via a prerecorded statement, on the quarterly earnings calls for shareholders.

By the end of the year, the company finally announced that Guy was leaving, but they left out a very juicy piece of information: I discovered that Guy had also been given $500,000 in severance. Ned and the board may have felt it was reasonable to buy Guy's silence at what I began to call "Nedbox," but it again spoke to the level of utter incompetence there. The culture of greed-induced backstabbing and betrayal was detrimental to Medbox and its shareholders.

Since the latter part of 2014, when control was hijacked away from me on the way to my dream of the NASDAQ, the share price had plummeted from fifteen dollars to about four cents by November 2015. The Ned-led board had taken on over $10 million of debt in exchange for free-trading shares at about half price. In public-company terminology, this is called "death-spiral financing," which is basically what it sounds like. They financed the company with horrible deals that crushed the market for its stock. I would never have engaged in these actions because I actually cared about the company and its shareholders. Exorbitant amounts of cash then went to high-priced attorneys, accountants, auditors, management, the board, and consultants.

Since my forced exile from the company, Ned and the board have issued more than twenty press releases about its promising future. Ironically, most of its touted successes were licenses I had helped file for on behalf of Medbox clients in Illinois, Nevada, Washington, Oregon, and California, granted only after I was gone.

The company has very little to show for the over $10 million financed with its stock as a commodity, to the detriment of shareholders. To make matters worse, the company's new management stopped honoring just about every contractual obligation to past clients, basically saying it didn't recognize them. If there was new money to be made off a contract, it was a different story. We never had that culture at Medbox before the Ned-led management took control. That kind of position with clients tarnishes your brand and reputation. This is especially true in the cannabis industry, where word travels fast and credibility can be ruined overnight. The Ned-led board and management team didn't care about that, because they had their scapegoat. Past clients would call me to complain about dishonored contracts, which the new management actually told them were part of the "Vince mess." Those were the "lucky" clients that got responses at all. That makes my blood boil! I voiced my concerns, but Nedbox did nothing to fix the issues. Ned wanted the company to start from scratch.

In mid-2015, I received word from my attorneys that the company's board was debating changing its name, and I joked to them that Nedbox would be apropos. Keeping a sense of humor truly saved me from going insane. What Ned didn't foresee was my ability to survive even in the direst of circumstances. Every move he made, even after he had control of the company, was meant to push me over the edge. He wouldn't want me to live to tell the tale, but he didn't get what he wanted. The greatest trick the devil ever pulled was convincing the world he doesn't exist.

I never compared anyone to the devil in my life before. Though people in positions of authority treated me poorly time and time again, I always saw them as just trying to get ahead by putting someone else down. That person isn't necessarily evil—just ambitious. I had managed to understand this clearly during all my trials and tribulations before dealing with Ned. Those who had targeted me in the past were no devils. Ned isn't really the devil either, but his actions were methodical, diabolical, calculating, and devilish.

In late 2014 and into 2015, I took a closer look at Ned's history as a businessman, his road to becoming a US ambassador to the Bahamas appointed by George W. Bush, and his business dealings concurrent with appointment as a director at Medbox. What I found wasn't at all shocking, but it shed a lot of light on the reasons for what happened at Medbox.

Ned is old money. His parents sent him off to become an attorney, but he left the practice of law and used the family fortune in Florida real-estate pursuits to make a name for himself. Notably, Ned was a lead plaintiff in a very important lawsuit that ultimately decided the US presidency in 2000 (*Siegel v. Lepore*). As many remember, "hanging chads" (referring to partially punched chads, or punch card ballots) were all over the news in November of 2000 after unclear election results left Al Gore and George W. Bush in a stalemate for the US presidency for months. Ned's lawsuit demanded that the initial count, which indicated a victory for George W. Bush, be upheld and that no manual recount take place of ballots that the automated counting process had not recognized.

Now, as a fan of NFL instant replay that ensures referees call plays accurately, I feel that anyone with a sense of justice would opt for a recount to ensure that something as serious as a presidential election is decided correctly. Obviously, Ned isn't a fan of due process, democracy, or fair dealing. Ultimately, his lawsuit prevented a recount, and George W. Bush became president. As is typical in politics, one favor was rewarded with another, and George W. Bush appointed Ned a US ambassador in October 2007. Ned is the kind of person who will do anything to win. As karma would dictate, however, Ned's ambassadorship was short-lived. After President Obama was elected, Ned had been ousted by the end of 2008.

In mid-2015, I fielded a call from Mitch Lowe, a Medbox director I had installed a couple of months before appointing Ned. Mitch, the co-founder of Netflix and ex-president of Redbox, is an incredible talent and rare entrepreneur, and he was one of the reasons that Ned didn't get to me at first. I had thought that Mitch wouldn't let anyone on that board have their way, but I was wrong.

The conversation was the first I had had with Mitch in almost a year. Medbox share value was in the pennies at that point under Ned's control, so I was dying to hear Mitch's news. He soon cut to the chase and said something unexpected—that he regretted that he had let Ned have his way. He said, "Ned knows real estate, not public companies." I was stunned at his candor.

I simply stated, "I'm the biggest loser in all this, Mitch. I thought the board had independence, and I was wrong." Then we started talking about the flurry of class-action suits filed against Medbox and its directors, along with past and present management. He was obviously troubled by all of it, but as he knew, I had warned them all that lawsuits were coming if they continued to ostracize the founder and lay blame on prior management for matters that the board hadn't properly researched because Ned's agenda had rushed it. Just as in the hanging-chad scenario that Ned was at the center of, Ned had trumped justice at Medbox. Greedy attorneys and the shareholders they solicited had sued after the restated financials and other announcements. All of it could have been avoided had it not been for Ned's handiwork.

Mitch was on to Ned, but he remained on the board at Medbox as of November 2015. Jennifer, the former FBI director, had seemingly grown tired of Ned's antics and resigned from the board in September 2015.

Ned's track record with other public companies since he joined the Medbox board in 2014 is very telling. He is a purveyor of penny stocks! He accepts director appointments at targeted public companies, and then, just as he did at Medbox, he calls prior financials into question, clears management out, and decimates the market for the company's stock. He appoints himself chairman and hires new attorneys, accountants, and auditors. With the market price in decline, he buys up the cheap stock and tries to rebuild its value so he can profit.

Does such a system sound way too brazen? I thought so too, but I connected the dots, and the facts became hard to ignore. Interestingly, Ned has yet to experience a rebound in share price for any of the companies he has destroyed, including Medbox. Here are some relevant statistics:

PositiveID Corp. [PSID]. Ned appointed February 2011. Stock Price: $0.55
Stock Price as of November 2015: $0.03
Ned's purchases: 631,076 shares at $0.03

Healthwarehouse.com, Inc. [HEWA]. Ned appointed June 2013. Stock Price: $1.88
Stock Price as of November 2015: $0.12
Ned's purchases: 113,543 shares at $0.22 and 83,333 shares at $0.30

Viscount Systems, Inc. [VSYS]. Ned appointed April 2014. Stock Price: $0.12
Stock Price as of November 2015: $0.01
Ned's purchases: 110,000 shares at $0.09 and 80,645 shares at $0.06

Medbox, Inc. [MDBX]. Ned appointed April 2014. Stock Price: $26.33
Stock Price as of November 2015: $0.06
Ned's purchases: 518,444 shares at $0.20

VeriTeq Corp. [VTEQ]. Ned appointed June 2014. Stock Price: $139.40 (adj. close)
Stock Price as of November 2015: $0.17
Ned's purchases: Unreported

CHAPTER 14

— ❧ —

With Pineapple Express, I Am Reborn

No matter what you're going through, there is always light at the end of the tunnel. You just need to find the light and keep the positive influences around you, close to you.

THE YEAR 2015 started out rough for me. I was out of a job. The company I had built from scratch was in the hands of others who, in my opinion, didn't care about the company or its shareholders. I was the subject of about a dozen lawsuits filed by shareholders of Medbox, whom I had never met or had any business dealings with. The SEC was actively investigating me for impropriety. Medbox owed me about $700,000 in loans from 2014. Characteristically, the Ned-led board kept delaying payment on those notes despite promises of promptness. All of this was simultaneous, causing tremendous financial and emotional hardship for me. I was close to giving up.

I then realized something that saved me from drowning. I could create a new business that was better and bigger. This time I knew what, and particularly whom, to avoid while building and maintaining value. However, my reputation had taken a beating from self-serving short-and-distort hit pieces from bloggers. Even the Medbox shareholder lawsuits quoted these articles as if they were fact, adding that I was a "criminal" and an "Iranian immigrant." It all left me a bit shell-shocked.

All the lawyers I needed to defend myself, plus a $34,000-per-month mortgage on a house I had purchased when I was still wealthy, had me reeling financially. I had been through hell and back yet still had a formidable mountain to climb with the equivalent of a bad foot and no equipment. I needed to do this on my own, with no support or safety net, as I had done with Medbox years earlier.

I looked for liquidity options. Though I had resisted selling Medbox stock before, I needed to survive. My holdings were still worth about $50 million. A cannabis business-investment firm that wanted to buy my majority interest in Medbox approached me. I structured a deal in early 2015 that would net me millions personally and would also bring millions in capital to the company on very favorable terms. If I was going to exit as majority shareholder, I wanted to make sure that the company was in good financial shape moving forward. I would still retain millions of shares and hopefully benefit from a rebound in Medbox's stock price when the company received my capital and had a new majority shareholder with industry experience at the helm. But the deal dragged on for months, and at the end of the day, it didn't fund. The investment-firm principal told me he was having a tough time dealing with Ned. Go figure!

I kept myself busy in the first half of 2015, founding a new consulting firm called MJ Business Consultants. In a way, I was going back to my roots. I had hundreds of contacts and industry knowledge that was arguably better than that of any other consultant in the business. To help me build this new company, I brought on the former vice president at Medbox, Matthew Feinstein, as CEO and cofounder. I also hired my longtime friend and former field technician at Medbox, Jaime Ortega, as field manager. Last, I hired the former operations assistant at Medbox, Anya Mikhaylova, as project manager. I trusted these people, who, fortunately for me, had been tossed aside in the "Nedbox" transition.

I had a faithful team now, and I was determined to get things moving for the new company. I wanted to give each of my hires a vested interest in the business, so I offered them an equity buy-in within the new private company. So, we all became partners with varying interests in MJ Business Consultants. One of the bigger mistakes an entrepreneur can make is not giving enough vesting to the supporting cast that helps launch a company. If they are in on the ground floor, give them the upside potential so they really work hard as if the company were their own—because that way, it is.

The team and I started sniffing out deals within the industry using my superior contacts and accumulated knowledge. I also decided that to further cement myself as a relevant entrepreneur, I needed to invent something new, something more powerful than my prior inventions. It would address all the operational concerns that a cannabis-dispensary operator might have day-to-day and avoid what was not popular about the Medbox system. I wanted a new technology that wouldn't be compared to my Medbox dispensing system. I was determined not to end up as a flash in the pan. The thought of being an irrelevant has-been at the age of thirty-six scared me to death. I commenced working on a prototype that I named Top-Shelf.

While I was busy developing Top-Shelf and pursuing ventures within the cannabis space to grow MJ Business Consultants into a powerhouse, I knew that even a viable private company and new invention could not recover the hundreds of millions of dollars of personal wealth and reputation that I had lost in the Medbox takeover. I decided to take a leap of faith and venture back into the public markets. I knew I just wouldn't be satisfied unless I made another public company successful after being shown the door publicly at Medbox.

I started looking into what Steve Jobs had gone through at Apple Computers in the mid-1980s and was shocked at the similarities in what we had gone through. His biography spoke of an inventor and entrepreneur that built a company from scratch, brought in a board and management team after the company gained notoriety, and then was shown the door by the people he put in charge in a very public manner. Although the similarities stop there—Jobs was a genius, and I am far from it—his story was powerful enough for me to realize a few things about success and failure. Anything short of regaining my well-deserved fortune and reputation was not acceptable for me, and I would spend the rest of my life angry over what had happened if I didn't at least try to regain my public-market lightning in a bottle. The fact that Ned would be watching me do it and grimacing at the thought of being shown up was just a cherry on top of the sundae. It also wasn't about the money but the philanthropic opportunities I would have missed out on because of my stolen legacy.

I strategized how we could take MJ Business Consultants public. I again considered a reverse merger, since I was savvy to the ins and outs of such a maneuver. But this time, I understood the importance of putting a solid team of accountants, auditors, attorneys, and professional advisors in place, who all had had spotless careers. I had had so much controversy swirling around me that I needed to surround myself with the right talent for the company to have any shot at success. I would again be the founder, majority shareholder, and technology consultant for the new company, but I would take steps to ensure that what I built was protected against what had happened at Medbox.

I sought the advice of counsel and put all my shares of the new company in a trust professionally managed by a licensed fiduciary. The account was then overseen by a law firm that specialized in drafting and protecting such trusts. The licensed fiduciary, or trustee, managed the affairs of the trust and sought guidance from the trust-protector firm when appropriate. The point was to take away any ammunition that my detractors might have (like shorters) to badmouth the new company because I was associated with it. I was simply too easy a target. I removed myself from an apparent position of control over the new company but would still be a part of its success. It was a winning strategy. The next step was finding the right publicly traded company to purchase a controlling stake in. After months of careful consideration, I identified my target.

Meanwhile, Medbox was absolutely tanking under Ned's dominion, as I had expected. Although I was somewhat happy that Ned couldn't resurrect what I had built after his calculated decimation of the company and its shareholder base, I was still majority shareholder. As Medbox stock began trading in the pennies, I realized that for some closure, I needed to give up being the majority shareholder and any perceived control I had of the company. I had had no actual control over Medbox for some time, and being its majority shareholder and founder no longer benefited me. It did nothing for my morale, business life, or public perception. My identity with that company had to be dissolved.

In early August 2015, I saw something shocking. Matt, our CEO at MJ Business Consultants, told me to look at the Medbox website. All of its content had been deleted. Pages of news articles, stories documenting the company's past triumphs for clients, and the corporate history of a once-successful company were replaced with the following:

> *Medbox, Inc., a leader in the rapidly emerging cannabis sector, provides specialized services to operators of dispensaries, cultivation centers, manufacturers and research facilities in those states where approved. Through trusted clients and affiliates, the company promotes efficient, consistent, high quality products that are priced right, readily available and safely packaged.*
> *(As of this writing, the site still carried this hapless, clumsy wording.)*

"The company promotes efficient, consistent, high quality products that are priced right, readily available and safely packaged"—so the company I once founded was now marketing and selling cannabis? Really? If not cannabis, then what, exactly? None of it made any sense.

I decided I would announce something that made waves. My August 2015 press release signaled my departure as majority shareholder for a company that I had founded but no longer recognized:

> *Medbox Founder & Majority Shareholder Retires 13 Million MDBX Shares for the Benefit of the Shareholders*
> *Founder Retires 2 Million Preferred Shares and 3 Million Common MDBX Shares Totaling 13 Million Shares and Also Announces New Venture Branded "Pineapple Express" Within Globestar Industries, Inc.*
> *LOS ANGELES, Aug. 26, 2015 (GLOBE NEWSWIRE)—P. Vincent Mehdizadeh, Founder and now former majority*

shareholder of Medbox, Inc. (OTCQB: MDBX) announced retiring
13 million shares of MDBX, including all 2 million preferred shares
in his possession, carrying 5 to 1 conversion to common shares
and super voting rights, along with an additional 3 million common shares. The shares have been retired, or in effect cancelled,
resulting in 13 million less shares issued and outstanding on a
fully diluted basis.

Mehdizadeh remains with approximately 11,778,746 common
shares of MDBX, of which he has transferred 1 million shares each
to Cannabis Policy Project (MPP) and Law Enforcement Against
Prohibition (LEAP). He has also pledged 3 million shares to a charity Mehdizadeh founded called Self-Made Foundation, Inc. That
transfer will occur after that nonprofit receives 501(c)(3) designa-
tion by the IRS. As a condition for receiving the gifts, the recipi-
ents have all agreed not to sell the gifted shares for a period of
one year and after the one year has elapsed, not to sell more than
40,000 shares per month.

"This share retirement is a token of my appreciation to the shareholders that made me proud to be associated with Medbox when
it was a leader in the cannabis sector," stated Vincent Mehdizadeh,
Founder and former majority shareholder of Medbox. "I am focused on a new venture now in 'Pineapple Express' (currently
known as Globestar Industries, Inc.), where I've taken my experiences at Medbox, which I haven't been a part of for over
a year now, and applied that knowledge to the new company.
Pineapple Express is laying a firm foundation in its development
stage by recruiting reputable accountancy advisors, top-tier legal
counsel, top-tier auditing support, and superior SEC compliance
and advisory talent at the board and officer level within the new
company. I am the Founder and Technology Advisor within that
company, which allows me to get back to my roots as an inventor

of compliance technology for the cannabis sector. I have placed my stock in that new venture, which represents the majority in that public company's issued and outstanding shares, in a trust which will be professionally managed by a licensed fiduciary as Trustee. This strategy allows me to focus on creating new technology without the riggers and responsibilities that majority shareholders have in managing company matters. I'm excited about the new venture and look forward to bringing long-term value to Pineapple Express shareholders through my creative inventions for many years to come."

About P. Vincent Mehdizadeh, Founder and Former Majority Shareholder at Medbox, Inc.

Mr. Mehdizadeh has been actively involved in the cannabis industry since 2008. Mr. Mehdizadeh is the founder of MJ Business Consultants, which is a subsidiary of "Pineapple Express"— Globestar Industries, Inc. (Pending name change to Pineapple Express, Inc.) At MJ Business Consultants Mr. Mehdizadeh serves as a senior advisor of technology development.

Mr. Mehdizadeh is considered an expert in the medical cannabis industry and is the inventor of two patents concerning the automated delivery of cannabis through a dispensing machine using biometric identification (Patent #US7844363) and a seed to sale POS system that tracks inventory and transactions occurring at cannabis dispensaries and cultivation facilities (Patent #US8818820). He is also the inventor of the patent-pending "Top-Shelf" System exclusively being developed for MJ Business Consultants. He has been interviewed and featured in news outlets including the Wall Street Journal, CNBC, FOX News, Bloomberg Businessweek, BBC, and many others.

Mr. Mehdizadeh was responsible for funding and the creation of the Cannabis Policy Project "Consume Responsibly" campaign, as well as the Americans For Safe Access "Medicate Responsibly" campaign aimed at educating medical and recreational cannabis users in the states that allow consumption of cannabis about its health effects and dosage information. Mehdizadeh has donated over $2 million dollars to Americans for Safe Access (ASA), Cannabis Policy Project (MPP), Drug Policy Alliance (DPA), Law Enforcement Against Prohibition (LEAP), and St. Jude Children's Research Hospital. Mehdizadeh has recently established a non-profit charitable foundation called Self-Made Foundation, Inc. and will continue his charitable contributions through that entity with his first project being an autobiography with all proceeds going to various charities.

The day before this announcement, I had issued a press release regarding my new venture that I had branded Pineapple Express. I had timed it to catch the attention of all the Medbox shareholders who still believed in me and my abilities. Hundreds of investors with whom I'd had direct contact with while growing Medbox into a powerhouse had benefited in the millions during my tenure. I was hoping that the market would take interest in my new endeavor, and fortunately, it did.

The press release announcing my new venture read as follows:

Globestar Industries Announces Share Exchange With Better Business Consultants, Inc. DBA MJ Business Consultants— Company Intends to Change Name to Pineapple Express, Inc.

Company to Apply for New Stock Symbol. Company Will Discontinue Any and All Prior Business of Globestar Industries Effective Immediately

LOS ANGELES, Aug. 25, 2015 (GLOBE NEWSWIRE)— Globestar Industries ("Globestar" or the "Company") (OTC

Pink: GSTI), a Wyoming corporation engaged in educational services, completed a share exchange on August 24th, 2015 with Better Business Consultants, Inc. DBA MJ Business Consultants ("MJB"), a California corporation. MJB specializes in cannabis industry consulting. Following the share exchange, the Company intends to change its name to Pineapple Express Inc. and apply for a new stock symbol. Effective immediately, all prior business of Globestar has ceased. MJB will continue on as a wholly-owned operating subsidiary of the Company.

Upon consummation of the share exchange:

All prior Globestar directors and officers resigned and MJB's Matthew Feinstein was appointed to serve as the sole director and officer until additional directors and officers, including an experienced Corporate Compliance Officer, are recruited for the public company.

100,500,000 shares of common stock, constituting approximately 99% of the Company's issued and outstanding stock, were cancelled and 50,000,000 new shares of common stock were issued to the four shareholders of MJB. These four shareholders are Matthew Feinstein, Anya Mikhaylova, Jaime Ortega and Sky Island Trust (held by PVM International, Inc. and to be transferred into the aforementioned trust).

$16,000 of debt owed to a former lender was extinguished.

"We are very excited to have completed this share exchange. We look forward to giving the public a comprehensive breakdown of all we have to offer in short order," commented Matthew Feinstein, CEO and Director of the Company. "We have a lot to offer the cannabis industry and I'm confident we have what it takes to be a relevant participant in the industry for years to come."

About the Company:

We are based in Los Angeles, California. Through our operating subsidiary Better Business Consultants, Inc. DBA MJ Business

Consultants, we plan to provide capital to our canna-business clientele, assume the role as landlord and lease properties to those canna-businesses, and provide consulting and technology to canna-businesses to develop, enhance, or expand existing infrastructures. We intend to create a nationally branded chain of cannabis retail stores under the "Pineapple Express" name as soon as federal laws allow, which will be supported by anticipated Company-owned cultivation and processing facilities, and will feature products from anticipated Company-owned manufacturers. As long as cannabis remains federally illegal our operations will be limited to consulting, product licensing, leasing to and investing in existing and new canna-businesses, selling industry specific technology, and providing ancillary support services. We believe that our competitive advantages include our wealth of experience, business model, exclusive proprietary technology, and key industry contacts in an industry that is foreign to most. It is our expectation that these factors will set us apart from most of our competitors.

"Nedbox" issued a letter to shareholders on September 1, 2015, showing that it was jealous, catty, or just plain irresponsible:

Last month, we announced an agreement between Medbox and a shareholder group led by the Company's founder, to retire all of the group's preferred shares and three million of its common shares, effectively relinquishing the group's majority voting position. The action had the effect of extending greater voting authority among all shareholders and should have a positive long-term impact on the Company's corporate structure.

I was blown away! The company's management and board were taking credit for my voluntary retirement of shares, which had been a complete and utter surprise to them. I immediately wrote Medbox's attorney, the board, and management and demanded they retract their unjust and categorically false statement about the origins and motivations of the share retirement. I threatened litigation immediately if the matter wasn't addressed appropriately. After an apology e-mail in which the release was called "an error," the company issued another release on September 4, 2015:

The Following Letter Was Sent to Vincent Mehdizadeh, Founder and Former Majority Shareholder Of Medbox, Inc. (OTCQB: MDBX) by the Company's President and Chief Executive Officer, Jeff Goh:

LOS ANGELES, CA / ACCESSWIRE / September 4, 2015 /
Dear Vince,
As Medbox moves forward in its next stage of growth and development, I want to personally extend my gratitude and thanks on behalf of the management team and board of directors.

Corporate transitions are always challenging. Please know that your recent voluntary cancellation and retirement of all of your Medbox preferred shares and three million of your common shares, effectively relinquishing a majority voting position, was very much appreciated as a benefit to the shareholders of Medbox.

As a management team, we are working hard and moving forward vigorously on a positive path to create a great company, pursuing solid business opportunities afforded by the burgeoning cannabis sector for the benefit of patients, as well as to meet our collective long-term goal of creating sustainable shareholder value.

I look forward to keeping you and all of our shareholders apprised of our progress.
Sincerely,
/s/Jeff Goh
Jeff Goh
President and Interim Chief Executive Officer

The public apology afforded me some closure. I didn't want to litigate against Medbox since it would distract me from Pineapple Express. Being spread too thin is a recipe for disaster for an entrepreneur. While Medbox had artfully worded the apology to limit its public embarrassment, it had served my purposes, and I let the matter go. I knew it was just another example I could point to of the folly of the "Nedbox" situation.

With Medbox firmly in my rearview, I focused fully on developing Pineapple Express to its potential. I happily announced my latest and greatest contribution to the cannabis industry...the Top-Shelf Safe Display System. The press release read as follows:

Pineapple Express, Inc. Announces Patent-Pending "Top-Shelf" System for Use in Cannabis

Unique Invention Combines 4 Critical Components Required of Canna-Businesses and Offers "Real-Time" Inventory Tracking and Increased Security

LOS ANGELES, Oct 6, 2015 (GLOBE NEWSWIRE)—Pineapple Express, Inc. (OTC Pink: PNPL) (the "Company"), a Wyoming corporation engaged in cannabis industry consulting, announced today that it has been assigned a patent application which is pending with the USPTO related to an invention called the "Top-Shelf" Display Safe System.

The patent-pending Top-Shelf Display Safe System (shown in the images above), exclusively developed for the Company by one of its founders, converts four critical components of the current dispensary model and combines them into a single, technologically advanced, and stylish unit. The system allows for a dispensary operator to do the following:

- *Safely and attractively display cannabis products,*
- *Secure all products in an armored exterior safe with interior locked compartments,*
- *Weigh all products in real-time using dozens of electronic scales housed in the locked compartments within the unit,*

- Transmit real-time inventory data to an integrated point-of-sale and inventory management system, and
- Authenticate transactions to consumers for legal compliance and record-keeping purposes.

The Company believes the Top-Shelf system could be the most powerful management tool available to cannabis dispensaries today. The system will also have the ability to work in concert with popular POS systems currently in use by dispensaries.

The Company has contracted with Pulse Design Group, an award-winning design firm with over 10 years of product design and manufacturing experience, to develop and produce the Top-Shelf system. The Company anticipates production and sales of the Top-Shelf system to commence in the first quarter of 2016 with a target retail price of $25,000. Lease and financing options will be made available to dispensaries on approved credit.

"The Company's Founder and Technology Consultant, Vincent Mehdizadeh, is the inventor of the Top-Shelf Display Safe System. He has been in the forefront of the legal cannabis industry since 2007 and has previously invented, patented, and developed other concepts related to secure dispensing and monitoring of cannabis at dispensaries and cultivation facilities. We are fortunate to have him create and develop new and exciting products for use in canna-businesses exclusively for Pineapple Express," stated Matthew Feinstein, CEO and Chairman. "After speaking with numerous dispensary owners all over the country, it became clear to me that Top-Shelf could address many issues present in today's dispensaries such as: protection from loss during burglaries and robberies, accurate transaction tracking, increased inventory management, and protection from internal theft and diversion. All this is achieved while not hindering the consumer experience at cannabis dispensaries. It is expected that the increased oversight and loss prevention achieved for a dispensary that uses Top-Shelf could save the dispensary thousands of dollars a year."

The Company will be offering the Top-Shelf system as part of its comprehensive branding and business development package available to every dispensary to which it provides consulting services or leases space. Eventually the Company envisions that the Top-Shelf system will be an integral part of the anticipated Pineapple Express branded Company-owned retail stores, when federal laws permit.

"Out of all my contributions to the cannabis industry, I'd have to say I'm most proud of this invention and its long-term implications," stated Mr. Mehdizadeh. "The first thing apparent when you walk into a dispensary is the jars of unsecure cannabis on display and prone to many risk factors for the dispensary, its operators, and also the consumers. Not only does this invention mitigate security and safety concerns, but it also uses electronic scales held in locked compartments within the unit that individually weigh the dispensary's inventory of cannabis products perpetually while keeping them out-of-sight and fully secure. The inventory data collected from the electronic scales is communicated back to the POS software after every dispensing transaction. The overwhelming benefits of the Top-Shelf system might be relevant to all demographics within the cannabis industry, such as: operators, consumers, state departments that regulate canna-businesses, industry advocates, and law enforcement. I am truly excited about the future of this invention."

I felt empowered! Again I had taken my lemons and made a gigantic jug of lemonade. This was my best invention yet. It solved so many issues that plagued cannabis dispensaries, and it was received well by shareholders, industry advocates, and my circle of contacts. The next few months were an absolute whirlwind of activity. My team and I at Pineapple Express were determined to make the company a breakout success. We issued the following letter to shareholders, documenting our milestones and activities since the merger that had made us a public company:

Pineapple Express, Inc. Provides Shareholder Update Letter

LOS ANGELES, Oct. 13, 2015 (GLOBE NEWSWIRE)— Pineapple Express, Inc. (OTC Pink: PNPL) (the "Company"), a Wyoming corporation engaged in cannabis industry consulting, (formerly known as Globestar Industries (OTC Pink: GSTI) today issued the following shareholder update letter from Matthew Feinstein, CEO and Chairman.

To our valued shareholders:

First and foremost, I wish to thank you for your continued support. As CEO of Pineapple Express, I am pleased to provide an update on the recent milestones we have achieved in our first full quarter of operations as Pineapple Express, and discuss our vision for the Company's future. I wish to take this opportunity to recount our recent corporate actions and business activities.

Pineapple Express has achieved substantive progress as we implement plans to create and capture shareholder value. To that end, we are pursuing an expansive growth and rollout program that leverages our integrated platform while capitalizing on our diverse opportunities across the United States. We expect the next six months to mark a major inflection point in our growth. To be sure, our best days are before us as we have amassed the right mix of talent and expertise to realize what we believe will be a promising future.

By way of review, Pineapple Express provides expert consulting, product licensing, and capital to help distinguish and grow new and existing businesses within the cannabis industry. In supplying industry specific technologies and ancillary support services, the Company provides a turnkey operating environment to canna-business managers. Pineapple Express is home to some of the most experienced and well-connected minds in the business, immediately placing its investors and clients at the forefront of an explosive industry. In fact, according to ArcView Market Research in their report "The State of Legal Cannabis Markets 3rd Edition, 2015," the cannabis industry was the fastest growing industry in all of the US in 2014.

Pineapple Express develops, enhances, and/or expands existing and newly formed infrastructures. Our business strategy is to quickly develop recurring and easily replicable revenue sources, and avoid large upfront investments in infrastructure, escalating payroll costs associated with expansion, and the years of initial losses often typical of start-up companies.

We believe that our unique business model, exclusive proprietary technology, expertise of our employees and consultants and our key industry contacts represent strong competitive advantages for Pineapple Express. We are pursuing a business model that we strongly believe positions us to capitalize on the evolving dynamics of the high-growth cannabis market space both before and after cannabis becomes federally legal. Currently, we are targeting opportunities in two distinct, yet symbiotic and complimentary markets, namely, the Licensed Medicinal Dispensary and Adult Use Cannabis Retail Market and the Licensed Cultivation, or Growers Market. We specifically provide capital to our canna-business clientele in these markets and we also purchase and lease real properties to these canna-businesses in states where canna-businesses are legal. In all cases, we offer consulting and technology to develop, enhance and/or expand existing and newly formed infrastructures and newly formed canna-businesses and we also offer high visibility and strongly branded product licensing. When cannabis becomes federally legal, we have provisions in our agreements with certain of our canna-business clients that allow us to buy their businesses and re-brand them as Pineapple Express locations, thus leveraging the strong brand appeal of our name.

This past quarter, the Company's common stock traded under new management on the OTC Pink Marketplace. We have made significant strides in shareholder value creation through our significant achievements in branding, management team and staff additions, business development, real property acquisition and the introduction of our proprietary "Top-Shelf" display safe system.

Recent Announcements and Milestones

I am excited to report on our recent developments and the milestones we have achieved. Below is a summary of our recent announcements:

On August 25, 2015 the Company announced its share exchange with Better Business Consultants, Inc. (dba MJ Business Consultants) and rebranding as Pineapple Express, Inc.

On August 26, 2015 the Company announced the appointment of Christopher Plummer as Chief Compliance Officer and Director. Mr. Plummer has over 16 years of regulatory compliance experience and his appointment shows our commitment to corporate compliance now and for the Company's expected future transition into a fully reporting company. The Company also announced key legal and accounting advisory engagements and intends to engage a new PCAOB registered public accounting firm in the near future.

On September 1, 2015 the Company announced that all employees, contractors, directors, officers, affiliates, and consultants for the company are subject to lockup agreements restricting them from selling any of their shares in the public markets for 2 years. This helps convey the company's priorities to the public markets and sets us apart from other publicly traded companies that are currently operating in and servicing the cannabis industry.

On September 8, 2015 the Company announced the signing of its very first property purchase and subsequent lease to a canna-business tenant.

On September 21, 2015 the Company announced its formal name change to Pineapple Express, Inc. and new ticker symbol: PNPL.

On September 24, 2015 the Company announced it retained CorProminence, LLC to provide investors relations and shareholder communications services.

On September 28, 2015 I conducted an audio interview about the Company with SmallCap Voice that can be heard by clicking here.

On October 6, 2015 the Company announced its development of a patent-pending system for use in cannabis dispensaries called the "Top-Shelf" display safe system that secures and weighs a dispensary's cannabis inventory in real-time before and after dispensing transactions through an integrated point-of-sale system operated by dispensary employees.

Branding

We believe the name "Pineapple Express" is extremely valuable and has an inherent value from which we can benefit. In our opinion, it will prove to be one of our best assets in establishing a lasting presence in the market and in the consumer's mind that will attract and retain customers.

Proprietary Product Development

Among our most notable achievements to date is our acquisition of proprietary technology, the patent-pending Top-Shelf display safe system. The Top-Shelf display safe system was exclusively invented and developed for the Company by co-founder and technology consultant Vincent Mehdizadeh. The Top-Shelf Display Safe System converts four critical components of the current dispensary model and combines them into a single, technologically advanced and stylish unit. The system allows for a dispensary operator to safely and attractively display cannabis products, secure all products in an armored exterior safe with interior locked compartments, weigh all products in real-time using dozens of electronic scales housed in the locked compartments within the unit, transmit real-time inventory data to an integrated point-of-sale and inventory management system, and authenticate transactions to consumers for legal compliance and record-keeping purposes. The Company believes the Top-Shelf system could be the most powerful management tool available to cannabis dispensaries today. The system will also have the ability to work in concert with popular POS systems currently in use by dispensaries. The Company is targeting Q1 2016 for commencement of product marketing and sales.

Initial Strategy Execution

We are especially excited to have executed our first property purchase and subsequent sublease to a canna-business tenant in California We are scheduled to receive rental income of $49,000 per month in year one, $98,000 per month in year two, and $122,500 in years three through ten from the subtenant, although actual rent received may vary and payment cannot be guaranteed.

The Company is also in late stage discussions and negotiations with several other parties to advance the execution of the model which include:

A proposed acquisition of a popular clothing brand and website. This potential acquisition includes a valuable URL address, a branded clothing line, a clothing distribution facility, and the rights to sell clothing, namely T-shirts, hats, beanies, pants, shorts, baseball jerseys, jackets, sweatshirts, polo shirts, and sweat pants displaying a popular industry specific trademarked name and logo.

Proposed relationship with Nature's Treatment of Illinois, Inc. ("NTI"), a dispensary located in Milan, Illinois in which management has a founding interest. NTI has been awarded one of the 60 dispensary licenses issued in Illinois. Construction has just started on the freestanding dispensary operation that is expected to open in early 2016.

Proposed investment in dispensary. The Company recently entered into a non-binding term sheet and is in the process of executing a definitive agreement to invest, expand, and co-brand an existing licensed dispensary in Vallejo, California, which has been in operation since 2010. The term sheet proposes a $600,000 investment and management support of the dispensary in exchange for 18% of gross revenue generated from the dispensary paid as a royalty and payment of consulting fees on an ongoing basis. The term sheet also provides for a buy-out clause of three times earnings for the business at the Company's option after three years and if recreational legislation is passed in California. Management is strongly optimistic that it has positioned the Company to capitalize on the high growth segments of the burgeoning cannabis markets. The landscape for growth is firmly rooted in the advancing market dynamics, industry trends and evolving federal and state drug policies. ArcView Market Research recently reported in their "The State of Legal Cannabis Markets 3rd Edition, 2015" research report that "...five states now boast markets greater than $100 million, while one additional state posted sales above the $50 million mark. With innovation occurring in delivery systems, healthier and easier alternative delivery formats are rapidly gaining market share. Opportunities are growing for multistate licensing with strong national cannabis brands finding ways to emerge in a state-segmented market. There are also very positive developments occurring regarding Quality Assurance and Quality Control and Product Testing with product potency and contaminant testing requirements emerging to ensure consumer safety and new laboratories emerging to support these needs. Cannabis brands are no longer hiding in the shadows and the branding bar is rising fast. The landscape of cultivation is evolving as well as licensed cultivation facilities are growing in size, creating opportunities and challenges to meeting their acreage needs and the fast growing demand for legal cannabis."

Capital Structure, Reporting/Uplisting Plans

Pineapple Express currently has 53.7 million shares outstanding as of 9/30/15. Our authorized capital stock consists of 500 million shares of common stock and 20 million shares of preferred stock, with 5 million shares of preferred stock designated as Series A Convertible Preferred Stock, of which 1.5 million shares are outstanding.

We intend to take all the steps necessary to become a fully reporting company in 2016 and potentially uplist to a national stock exchange in the years that follow. Our most recent interim report filed with the OTC Markets on September 16, 2015 can be found here.

New Website

We are delighted to report that we have secured www.pineappleexpress.com as our main corporate website domain and we will be launching our new corporate website on November 1, 2015. In addition to a comprehensive description of our products *and services and related content, our website will provide links to our financial statements, corporate governance policies, stock price and share information, complete press release coverage, relevant corporate filings, media, events calendar and a sub-scriber option to receive automatic email alerts upon the issu-ance of future press releases and filings. We will be releasing further information regarding the launch of the new website in the coming weeks.*

On behalf of the entire Pineapple Express management team, I would like to again thank you for your continued support. In closing, we strongly believe that we have the talent, expertise and strategic approach necessary to create the future we envi-sion and we look forward to reporting on our excellent progress as we continue to execute on our ambitious plans.

Sincerely,

Matthew Feinstein, CEO and Chairman, Pineapple Express Inc.

The feeling around company headquarters was productive and calming for me. I had surrounded myself with talented professionals who respect-ed me for my business prowess and determination to right all that had gone wrong for me at Medbox. All of them had witnessed the Ned take-over, and we were all filled with anger channeled in the right way. We all felt we had something to prove, but none more than I.

However, while I was keeping myself busy building the new company, I was facing something I hadn't in years. I was running out of money. Attorney bills began to pile up, my monthly expenses were high, and Pineapple Express needed more and more cash to continue the com-pany's growth. Besides about a million dollars in Medbox stock that I had left, all I had was the equity in my house at about $3.5 million. I had listed it for sale in April 2015, but seven months later as I write this, it still has not sold.

The shareholder lawsuits against Medbox that had named me were going to crush me financially. My attorneys had quoted me upward of $2 million for my defense over the next couple of years. If my house didn't sell, I would be in dire straits, and my vision for Pineapple Express would never come to pass. A broke company founder is tantamount to a blind ship's captain. Then I caught a break. I attended a mediation regarding all the shareholder lawsuits, which was certainly interesting. Imagine me, with my two attorneys, walking into a room of about thirty attorneys representing Medbox, the board, prior and current management, and the aggrieved shareholders I had never met or had any business dealings with. It was something to behold.

The mediator, who was a retired federal judge, sequestered all the parties in different rooms, which took up the entire floor of an office building. He made the rounds of the rooms to talk with each party. When he entered our room, I approached him and we shook hands. As he looked deeply into my eyes, I remained calm and unbothered; I did not find him intimidating. I answered his questions truthfully and candidly. What was I willing to contribute to resolve all cases? I stated that I was considering countersuing all the plaintiffs and their attorneys for filing frivolous cases against me. He was taken aback. I then spent about twenty minutes qualifying my response, explaining to him all that had occurred. I said, "Your Honor, I was the victim of a corporate hijacking by the people I myself appointed to the board."

I told him that I had always acted under the advice of counsel, especially after Medbox's tremendous success, and I explained all the things I had done to protect shareholders and grow the company until I was forced out. He understood my position and said he would talk to the other parties. My attorneys cautioned me that the chances of the case settling at mediation were slim to none. I said I was optimistic.

After we sat there for hours, the mediator came back. He said that he understood that I didn't want to contribute any cash but suggested that I could contribute shares. He added, "I think I can get this wrapped up today." My stunned attorneys immediately perked up. I reflected over the past couple of months. I had just retired thirteen million shares and given two million more to charity. What would I give now to get rid of frivolous cases that had hurt my morale and were actively harming my business reputation, decimating my finances, and potentially hurting Pineapple Express?

I offered two million shares—my best and final offer. The shares were worth about $120,000 at the time, the equivalent of one month of legal-defense fees. It was a no-brainer for me. A no-cash settlement would be an absolute personal vindication and victory. In addition, it was a business decision. I would be left with about eight million Medbox shares that would presumably increase in value once the settlement of the shareholder lawsuits was announced to the public. After another hour, the mediator returned to the room with my attorneys and said, "It's done."

My attorneys were in shock—not because they felt I was at fault, but because, as they explained, this type of walk-away settlement simply doesn't happen in cases like this. It was a surreal experience to walk out of the mediation with my head held high, past all those attorneys who had been unfairly gunning for me for those many months. Keeping to my roots, I rushed home to author a press release that was therapeutic and cathartic. The language in the civil complaints the attorneys had filed for the shareholders had been racially charged and extremely derogatory about me and my ethnicity. Everyone has heard of African Americans being racially profiled by police officers and getting a "DWB"—driving while black. Well, I was officially guilty of an "SWP"—succeeding while Persian—in the minds of these plaintiffs' attorneys. My attorney advised me to hold off the release until after the ink was dry on the settlement documents. It read as follows:

Medbox Founder Comments on Pending Dismissal of All Shareholder and Derivative Lawsuits
    Pending dismissals and zero cash settlements achieved by Founder on shareholder class actions and derivative matters
    LOS ANGELES, December 7, 2015 (GLOBENEWSWIRE)—P. Vincent Mehdizadeh, Founder and former majority shareholder

of Medbox, Inc. (OTCQB: MDBX) commented on the pending dismissal of the shareholder and derivative lawsuits filed against Medbox, Inc.

"From the onset of these legal matters I have been vocal about the inaccurate and inflammatory statements contained in these lawsuits about my character and my management of Medbox matters when I was in a position of control at that company," stated Vincent Mehdizadeh, Founder and former majority shareholder of Medbox. "The complaint itself made very derogatory racial statements about my heritage as an 'Iranian immigrant' and a 'criminal.' I am happy that all lawsuits are being dismissed and resolved without my contribution of any cash to the derivative or shareholder plaintiffs in those matters. At all times I was in an earnest pursuit to operate the most ethical and professional companies in the cannabis sector and as a result recruited a seasoned management team and high-profile board of directors to help lead the way. In retrospect, that decision didn't work out for the company as I had hoped. Resolving these claims in the manner they were ultimately resolved, prior to the class even being certified by the court, and with zero cash payment by me to the class and derivative plaintiffs, demonstrates a clear and convincing personal victory."

Mehdizadeh contributed 2 million shares to the derivative class as part of the global settlement.

Mehdizadeh added, "My contribution of 2 million shares to the derivative class, with a current value of about $40,000, was necessary to get the cases resolved for the benefit of the company and its shareholders. A few months ago, I voluntarily retired 13 million shares for the benefit of the shareholders and donated another 2 million shares to charity. Contributing these additional shares to get these matters resolved was a no-brainer. I am happy to report I have moved on from Medbox and have transitioned *to what I consider to be a better fit for my professional skills and talents."*

The dismissal of the lawsuits cleared my mind for developing the Pineapple Express business model. I have all the confidence in the world that I will take that company to the top and be a relevant force in the cannabis industry for years to come.

As for the SEC investigation into Medbox, it is still pending as of this writing. I am at the center of that for one key reason. Remember Phillip? He had asked something he never should have: "Where do you want these shares to go?" The shares in question were the 226,000 certificate shares that had been part of my Shannon buyout. I had assumed, as anyone might, that the attorney had proposed a procedure that was valid, legal, and beyond reproach. Well, my kind gesture in coordinating the transfer of those shares to my then-girlfriend, under Phillip's supervision, was a mistake that ended up costing me dearly. The correct procedure was to add the shares to what I already held as majority shareholder or just cancel them, as I had done with millions of other shares received in the Shannon buyout. Phillip's mistake cost me my legacy with Medbox and gave Ned the tools to execute on his agenda.

While I have an ironclad defense of unknowingly following an attorney's bad advice, my current attorneys tell me that these investigations can drag on for years. I was not aware that Phillip's advice was bad until years later, when skilled SEC attorneys told me. I could never have imagined that it would mean losing my company. The take-away for aspiring entrepreneurs is that you are only as strong as the attorneys advising you. Question everything. Don't think that a law degree and membership in the bar prove that someone is competent. Clearly, some attorneys are not. Despite the bad legal advice and an unscrupulous board member torpedoing my legacy at Medbox, I am more motivated than ever to build a new legacy for myself at Pineapple Express!

Here are my predictions. By 2018, I'll be worth hundreds of millions of dollars again through the forty-two million Pineapple Express (PNPL) shares held in trust on my behalf. The federal government will have removed cannabis from the list of Schedule I substances (those that have no currently accepted medical use in the United States). California will follow Oregon, Washington, Colorado, Alaska, and the District of Columbia in becoming a recreational-cannabis state. I will have donated an additional $2 million to charities and also furthered my own charity, Self-Made Foundation Inc., which focuses on community outreach and providing grants to disadvantaged and low-income entrepreneurs. Last, the criminal convictions will be expunged from my record, and I'll have a clean slate. While it's true that "a successful man is one who can lay a firm foundation with the bricks others have thrown at him," it's also true that avoiding the bricks in the first place is better.

What am I? I have the mind of an inventor, spirit of an entrepreneur, heart of a philanthropist, and soul of an artist. I am all those things wrapped in one uniquely imperfect being that has suffered through his mistakes and continues to grow as a person and entrepreneur every day.

I realize this book could potentially make me even more of a target. Ned obviously has friends in high places, and Medbox investigations are still ongoing; investigations which were exacerbated by the "Nedbox" corporate hijacking that occurred at my expense. However, I will never back down, and I will never lie down. The truth should always be voiced no matter how difficult. I've come too far and I will not lose... ever. My life's saga continues...

ꝓ

Afterword

A NOTE TO other aspiring entrepreneurs:

People can achieve their dreams if they put their hearts and souls into it. You don't necessarily need a top-notch education to succeed in this world. A good education is obviously preferable, but it's not required. If all the chips are down and you can't receive a higher education, you can still have an amazing life.

People spend a fortune going to school and postgraduate school. Bogged down in student loans, they spend their whole lives behind the eight ball, trying to pay off their debt. A lot of my friends grew up with comfortable lives, and their parents paid for their educations. I didn't have that luxury. Yet, I have made a success of my life.

Never let anyone else determine the viability of your idea. If you believe you can benefit an industry or consumers, refuse to let others distract you from your chosen path or keep you from success.

Remember the crab-bucket mentality: "If I can't have it, neither can you." *Wikipedia* defines it this way:

Individually, the crabs could easily escape from the pot, but instead, they grab at each other in a useless "king of the hill" competition which prevents any from escaping and ensures their collective demise. The analogy in human behavior is that members of a group will attempt to "pull down" (negate or diminish the importance of) any member who achieves success beyond the others, out of envy, conspiracy, or competitive feelings.

Sadly, plenty of people think this way. I am motivated by the love of calling out people like that. It is one of my great joys in life.

There are more spectators than doers, more onlookers than movers and shakers. Think of it this way: if you're an entrepreneur who is pursuing your dream, you're in the gladiator ring. The mob watching you is fickle by nature. You are in ancient Rome, before the emperor—or today, and you're before the federal government—and he is a spectator, too. Some in the crowd support you, but plenty of angry and envious people bet on you to lose.

Being successful means more than just achieving success. You have to maintain it and avoid becoming jaded by it. Every single experience I've had has humbled me. So many things had to align for me to achieve greatness each time, which is where I now find myself. I never take that for granted. I feel blessed and humbled to be in a position to pay it forward. Every day, I aspire to live up to the blessings I've received. I constantly push myself to become a better person in mind, body, and spirit.

I didn't have life handed to me, but I don't know if I'd be where I am today if it weren't for everything that happened. Even my scrapes with the law helped set the stage for where I am. When I take that perspective, I don't really regret the past.

I have only one regret in life: not spending more time with my mother. She was a wonderful person, and she needed to be nurtured and looked after more. The entire family failed her. I spent time with her and supported her financially. But, while I made an effort, I could have done more. Otherwise, I don't regret the mistakes I've made because I've learned from them. Every once in a while, before I go to sleep, I thank the universe for my many blessings, and I thank my mother for looking out for me in the afterlife and ask her to keep looking out for me.

I believe firmly in destiny. I also believe that we each control our paths in life. I believe that we have multiple paths, all predetermined. When you're born, each of your possible paths branch off into ten others, and so on and so forth, like the branches of a tree. The path you end up on depends on each unique decision—going to college or not, or doing this, not that. The branches don't intertwine or tangle. Many outcomes could result; our choices dictate which of our predetermined paths we take.

Out of the need to take care of my family, I turned creative and developed a product—the Medbox. Then, out of the need to save myself from financial ruin, I created another product, the Top-Shelf, and the vision for Pineapple Express. I am a living example of necessity being the mother of invention.

Patience, perseverance, intuition, ambition, and a little bit of luck—at the end of the day, I don't measure my success based on my net worth. I instead look at the hundreds of investors I've gotten to know since founding Medbox in 2010. Every single one has made many times an initial investment in me and my ideas. We are talking about hundreds of people making millions of dollars. That translates into paid-off credit-card bills and mortgages and funded college tuitions. That kind of positive impact on people's lives is what I believe is my greatest accomplishment. That is my true legacy, and I expect to do the same at Pineapple Express.

Made in the USA
San Bernardino, CA
08 June 2016